CITIZENSHIP AND DEMOCRACY IN SCHOOLS
DIVERSITY, IDENTITY, EQUALITY

CITIZENSHIP AND DEMOCRACY IN SCHOOLS
DIVERSITY, IDENTITY, EQUALITY

Edited by Audrey Osler

Trentham Books
Stoke on Trent, UK and Sterling, USA

Trentham Books Limited

Westview House	22883 Quicksilver Drive
734 London Road	Sterling
Oakhill	VA 20166-2012
Stoke on Trent	USA
Staffordshire	
England ST4 5NP	

First published 2000

British Library Cataloguing-in-Publication Data
A catalogue record for this book is available from the British Library

1 85856 222 8 (paperback)

The cover photograph is by Terry Wrigley and was taken at Rushey Mead Secondary School in Leicester. We thank headteacher Steve White for permission to use the picture and Terry Wrigley for his generousity in letting us use his work on this book, although he took it while researching his own book, The Power to Learn; stories of success in the education of Asian and other bilingual pupils *(Trentham, 2000).*

Designed and typeset by Trentham Print Design Ltd., Chester and printed in Great Britain by Cromwell Press Ltd., Wiltshire.

Contents

Introduction • 9
Audrey Osler

PART ONE: THE CITIZENSHIP AGENDA

Chapter 1
Citizenship, Human Rights and Cultural Diversity • 13
Audrey Osler and Hugh Starkey

Chapter 2
**The Implications of the Human Rights Act
for Citizenship Education** • 19
Sarah Spencer

Chapter 3
Children's Rights and Education • 33
Eugeen Verhellen

PART TWO: RACE, IDENTITY AND HUMAN RIGHTS

Chapter 4
Citizenship Education for a Plural Society • 47
Peter Figueroa

Chapter 5
Human Rights, Cultures and Language Teaching • 63
Michael Byram and Manuela Guilherme

Chapter 6
**Human Rights and Racial Justice:
connections and contrasts** • 79
Robin Richardson

Chapter 7
**Human Rights, Responsibilities and
School Self-Evaluation** • 91
Audrey Osler and Hugh Starkey

PART THREE: PRACTISING DEMOCRACY

Chapter 8
**Implementing Citizenship Education in a
Primary School** • 113
David Brown

Chapter 9
Practising Democracy in two Inner City Schools • 125
Priscilla Alderson

Chapter 10
Democratic Practice in a Secondary School • 133
Jeremy Cunningham

Chapter 11
Schools, Democracy and Violence in South Africa • 143
Clive Harber

Chapter 12
**Meeting the Challenge of Inclusion: human rights
education to improve relationships in a boys'
secondary school** • 151
Charlotte Carter

Chapter 13
'Race', School Exclusions and Human Rights • 161
Maud Blair

CONTENTS

Chapter 14
**The Children's Parliament in Rajasthan:
a model for learning about democracy** • 169
Mary John

Chapter 15
The Role of Black Governors • 177
Ian Gittens

Chapter 16
Parents, Human Rights and Racial Justice • 185
Seán Carolan

Chapter 17
**The Control of Educational Democracy:
international perspectives** • 193
Lynn Davies

Note on Contributors • 213

Index • 215

Acknowledgements

I wish to thank a number of individuals and organisations who have supported me in the preparation of this book.

The Economic and Social Research Council for funding the research seminar series *Human Rights and Democracy in Schools* (grant no: R451 26 4599 97) from which this book has developed.

The Council of Europe and particularly the Directorate of Human Rights, for providing technical support to the seminar series. Thanks to Stefano Valenti and to Maggie Nicholson.

The Universities of Birmingham and Leicester and the Open University for hosting the seminars.

The Commission for Racial Equality, the Citizenship Foundation, the Runnymede Trust, the 1990 Trust and Charter 88 and all those individuals who took part in the seminar series.

The Education in Human Rights Network and Birmingham Development Education Centre for organising a teachers' conference in May 1998, also entitled *Human Rights and Democracy in Schools*, which coincided with the launch of the seminar series. The conference allowed a number of contributors to this book to present their research in workshops for teachers and to engage in debate with Professor Bernard Crick, the Chair of the Government's Advisory Group, Education for Citizenship and the Teaching of Democracy in Schools. Particular thanks to Seán Carolan, Ina Clason and Scott Sinclair.

Special thanks to Judy Dandy for her part in organising the seminar series and the teachers conference. And to Dr Hugh Starkey and Samantha Keenan for their assistance in the editorial processes.

The editor and publishers also wish to thank the editors of *Prospects* for their agreement to use material from Eugeen Verhellen, Children's Rights and Education 39(2). Also, the editors of *Multicultural Teaching* for use in chapter one of material adapted from Audrey Osler, Citizenship democracy and political literacy 18(1): 12-15 and 29.

Introduction

Audrey Osler

This book is designed both for the general reader and as a key text for courses in citizenship education aimed at both new and experienced teachers. The contributors include researchers, teachers and headteachers with wide-ranging experience of initiatives to promote learning for citizenship and democracy in primary and secondary schools, working with colleagues, students, parents and school governors. These articles and reports highlight examples of successful practice, but also discuss some of the challenges and difficulties. All those interested in or responsible for citizenship education will find practical and thought-provoking ideas in these accounts.

The title, *Citizenship and Democracy in Schools: diversity, identity, equality* summarises the main themes of the intense discussions which took place from 1998-2000 in a seminar series funded by the Economic and Social Research Council and entitled *Human Rights and Democracy in Schools*. This volume brings together the contributions of a number of the participants in those seminars. The seminar series coincided with the passing of the Human Rights Act 1998 which incorporates the European Convention on Human Rights into UK law and which aims to establish a culture of human rights in the UK.

At the launch of the seminar series the Government's Advisory Group on *Education for Citizenship and the Teaching of Democracy in Schools* had just published its initial report. This provided seminar participants with an opportunity to discuss their research findings in the context of its recommendations. We were also able to invite the Chair of the Advisory Group, Professor Bernard Crick, to a teachers' conference, organised by the Education in Human Rights Network, also entitled *Human Rights and Democracy in Schools*. This enabled us to engage Professor Crick in a dialogue about the place of human rights within education for citizenship and to contribute directly to the Advisory Group's consultation process.

One of the original objectives of the seminar series was to explore the relationship between human rights education and initiatives to promote race equality. Our research and discussions were given particular impetus by the publication in February 1999 of the Stephen Lawrence Inquiry report (Macpherson *et al*, 1999), and the subsequent Government plan of action (Home Office, 1999) which included three specific recommendations on the role of education in preventing and addressing racism.

The ESRC seminar series allowed our research to be scrutinised by colleagues working in schools, local education authorities and non-governmental organisations. Our debates were particularly enriched by contributions which drew on experiences from various parts of Britain, Northern Ireland and the Republic of Ireland. We also benefited from the participation of a number of international research students and colleagues who joined us from other parts of Europe, Australia, Japan and the USA.

In Part One, *The Citizenship Agenda*, we situate the introduction of Citizenship to schools in England within a wider debate about the development of a vision of multicultural Britain within a multicultural Europe. Chapter one examines issues of identity in the context of a society characterised by diversity and inequalities and re-examines some essential features of a politically literate citizen. In chapter two Sarah Spencer considers the relationship between citizenship education, human rights and the development of a human rights culture. In particular she draws out some implications of the Human Rights Act for citizenship education in schools. The chapter provides lively examples of how schools in other parts of the world educate for human rights in ways which are relevant to the lives of young children and adolescents. Chapter three draws on the legislative framework of the UN Convention on the Rights of the Child, to explore changing constructs of childhood. Eugeen Verhellen calls on teachers to consider the implications for schools of recognising children as current citizens with participation rights rather than citizens in waiting.

Part Two is entitled *Race, Identity and Human Rights*. Peter Figueroa presents us with a model of citizenship education for a plural society which brings together four key elements. He argues that it is essential to combine philosophical analysis with social analysis and historical understanding and that any programme of education for citizenship must also address the particular culture of the school. Within his model, citizenship education is integrated with human rights education, multiculturalism and antiracism. In the following chapter Michael Byram and Manuela Guilherme build upon this understanding of cultural pluralism, arguing that foreign language teachers have a key role in extending the notion of a plural model of citizenship and identity to an international level. They explore the interaction of human rights and the teaching and learning of language-and-culture, suggesting that foreign language-and-culture education can contribute significantly to both human rights and citizenship education. Robin Richardson develops the debate by posing some challenging questions to human rights educators from a race equality perspective. This section ends with Audrey Osler and Hugh Starkey returning to the theme of a human rights culture, this time with a focus on a global culture of human rights. We consider how schools assess the progress they have made in developing a culture of rights and conclude by examining the relationship between human rights and responsibilities, and the continuing pedagogic challenge of identifying and promoting responsibilities linked to rights.

Part three, *Practising Democracy*, draws on the contributions of both researchers and teachers to illustrate how schools are educating children and young people for democracy and citizenship. David Brown begins by discussing how a school might begin to implement citizenship education, drawing on his experience as a primary headteacher and on the particular context of his own school, which he describes as being at an 'embryonic' stage in its development for citizenship education. Priscilla Alderson follows with reports of two primary schools which have taken particular steps to become more democratic, in response to concerns about discipline and inclusion. From his vantage point as a secondary headteacher, Jeremy Cunningham reflects on various initiatives in which he has engaged to encourage democratic practice. He highlights some successes and points out that in practising democracy, both students and teachers will inevitably make mistakes. He stresses the importance of coping with these mistakes as an essential part of developing genuine democratic practice.

Clive Harber presents two further case studies of democratic practice in schools, this time from South Africa. He concludes that schools in South Africa are not helpless in the face of violence and that education for democracy can play an important part in helping to combat violence. In the following chapter Charlotte Carter also examines the theme of conflict and reports on her efforts to improve relationships in a boys' secondary school by using intervention strategies which utilise a human rights education framework. She draws on students' own reflections to argue that even in adverse circumstances an individual teacher can work with groups of students to develop their sense of security, self-knowledge and understanding of human rights.

Maud Blair returns to the theme of how we construct images of childhood and relates it to the practice of expelling children from school. She argues that negative representations of black male youth in Britain have led directly and indirectly to denials of human rights in both the education and criminal justice systems. By way of contrast Mary John presents us with a positive model of democracy in practice which has challenged how communities perceive children. She reports on the practices of the Indian Children's Parliament in Rajasthan, demonstrating how the experience of democracy in action has empowered children to become responsible members of their communities, effectively challenging discrimination based on gender, caste and age.

Ian Gittens and Seán Carolan examine the potential and actual contributions of school governors and parents in studies which address democratic practice in the wider school community. In his study Gittens considers how black school governors might enhance the schools' provision and the learning opportunities open to students by exercising their own citizenship. Parents can also bring a fresh perspective to a school. In Carolan's study they emphasised the importance of human rights and antiracist education as essential elements in education for citizenship, in effect endorsing the model proposed by Figueroa.

The volume ends with a discussion, by Lynn Davies, of the degree to which governments need actively to plan and legislate for educational democracy. Drawing on a range of international examples, she develops a typology of intervention, arguing that democracy requires both the effective support of state institutions and a strongly supported civil society. She concludes that it is not enough that the State legislates to ensure that the minimum conditions for democracy are met, through mechanisms for student representation, equal rights and the resolutions of grievances. Nor is it sufficient that it sets out a framework for deliberative democracy or the discussion of controversial issues. It is also vital that both children and teachers *participate* in the political process, and that, as Cunningham also noted, they are able to learn from mistakes, if they are to become well-educated citizens.

References

Home Office (1999) *Stephen Lawrence Inquiry: Home Secretary's Action Plan.* London: Home Office.

Macpherson, W. *et al.* (1999) *The Stephen Lawrence Inquiry.* Report of an inquiry by Sir William Macpherson. London: The Stationery Office.

Part 1
The Citizenship Agenda

1

Citizenship, Human Rights and Cultural Diversity

Audrey Osler and Hugh Starkey

This chapter attempts to situate the introduction of Citizenship to schools in England, within a wider debate about the development of a vision of a multicultural Britain within a multicultural Europe. We have previously defined citizenship education as having two inter-related components, namely the structural/ political and the cultural/ personal (Richardson, 1996; Osler and Starkey, 1996). The former is clearly the field of Citizenship whilst the latter is also the concern of Personal, Social and Health Education (PSHE). Whilst the National Curriculum for England proposes a combined Citizenship and PHSE programme in the primary school, there are separate programmes of study at secondary level. We argue for a holistic approach at all levels. In other words the cultural and personal elements, which by definition involve the affective as well as the cognitive domains, must interact with all teaching and learning activities designed to promote knowledge and understanding.

The importance of such considerations becomes particularly acute when account is taken of the diversity within any society. The National Curriculum is a uniform framework, but those required to study it are a diverse group, not necessarily identifying easily or primarily with a particular nation, such as England. Indeed, attempting to define national characteristics for England is a quest notable for raising more questions than it answers (Paxman, 1998).

The concept of citizenship is founded on the notion of individual as actor in a democratic polity and this requires an understanding of and acceptance of human rights. Human rights provide the framework for political and social interaction in democracies by ensuring the equality of all individuals before the law and in respect of their rights to dignity and to the fundamental freedoms (thought, conscience and religion; association; expression; movement; holding property; marriage and family life) which constitute the bulwark against arbitrary actions by the state or its agents acting out of prejudice or malice.

Human rights were devised and accepted by the international community to preserve humanity from the catastrophic conflicts resulting from state sponsored racism. In the 1930s and 1940s this took the extreme form of fascist and nazi regimes. Racism has always been the major enemy of democracy and of liberal societies. The fact that institutional racism persists in liberal societies, including Britain even today, means that the whole basis of democracy and citizenship is constantly undermined (Macpherson *et al*, 1999). It is for this reason that we consider it essential to situate Citizenship and democracy in schools within a context of cultural diversity and therefore on the basis of human rights.

Citizenship in the school curriculum

At one level, the importance of a curriculum that is inclusive of cultural diversity is an accepted fact. One of the purposes of the National Curriculum for England is the establishment of an entitlement for all school children and the official commentary on this purpose makes specific reference to diversity and to citizenship:

> The National Curriculum secures for all pupils, irrespective of social background, culture, race, gender, differences in ability and disabilities, an entitlement to a number of areas of learning and to develop knowledge, understanding, skills and attitudes necessary for their self-fulfilment and development as active and responsible citizens. (DfEE/QCA, 1999b: 12)

Such assertions are not, however, sufficient to ensure that equality is given due consideration by schools, let alone achieved.

And yet, the introduction of Citizenship to the National Curriculum for England is the single most important element of the new, year 2000 edition of that curriculum. It provides a unique opportunity to promote education for racial equality. The UK Government has indeed highlighted citizenship education as a key means by which education for racial equality can be achieved (Home Office, 1999). Yet a number of commentators have questioned whether the National Curriculum generally and the new citizenship curriculum in particular, which is to be introduced into English schools from autumn 2000, can really support initiatives for racial equality (Ramsaran, 1999; Figueroa, 1999). We have previously highlighted the fact that the Crick Report *Education for Citizenship and the Teaching of Democracy in Schools* (QCA, 1998) in its representation of minorities and also in its discussion of identity and diversity falls short, in many ways, of a clearly situated human rights perspective (Osler 2000; Starkey 2000). A central concept of the Crick Report, namely political literacy, can nevertheless be built upon, given that a commitment to human rights principles and skills for challenging racism are essential features of a politically literate citizen within a democratic society.

Racism and the education system

Schools are a key means by which we can promote racial equality, yet they are also part of an education system in which institutional and inter-personal racism continues to flourish. The report of the Stephen Lawrence Inquiry defined institutional racism as:

> The collective failure of an organisation to provide an appropriate and professional service to people because of their colour, culture, or ethnic origin. It can be seen or detected in processes, attitudes and behaviour which amount to discrimination through unwitting prejudice, ignorance, thoughtlessness and racist stereotyping which disadvantage minority ethnic people. (Macpherson, *et al,* 1999: 28)

Examples of the effects of institutional racism within the education system have been well documented. They include the over-representation of black and other minority students among those excluded from school (Osler, 1997b; DfEE, 1999); differentials in educational outcomes between ethnic groups in many schools and local education authorities (Gillborn and Gipps, 1996; Richardson and Wood, 1999); the barriers to promotion and career progression which black and minority teachers may experience at each stage in their careers, whether they are in training, newly qualified, or holding headships or other senior positions (Osler, 1997a); the failure of the school inspections system to address adequately issues of race equality (Osler and Morrison, 2000).

Racism, democracy and citizenship education

Racism has been identified as a key force that serves to undermine democracy in Europe and one which therefore needs to be addressed through programmes in schools and in teacher education (Council of Europe, 1985). At the Council of Europe Vienna Summit held in 1993, Heads of State and Government, persuaded that 'manifestations of intolerance threaten democratic societies and their basic values' called for a

> ...broad European Youth Campaign to mobilise the public in favour of a tolerant society based on the equal dignity of all its members and against manifestations of racism, xenophobia, antisemitism and intolerance. (Council of Europe, 1993)

A number of other European-funded projects, involving educators from Britain, have explored how we might most effectively confront racism, xenophobia, gender inequality and other challenges to democracy and human rights through citizenship education. The *All different, All equal* campaign established in response to the 1993 Vienna Declaration resulted in the publication of useful materials (for example, Rothemund, 1995) which exploit the potential of peer education in challenging racist attitudes and intolerance amongst the young. The practical outcomes of another project addressing both teachers and teacher educators have been published and used in teacher education in Britain (Osler, Rathenow and Starkey, 1996; Holden and Clough, 1998). Citizenship education is seen across Europe as playing a central role in strengthening democracy and in challenging racism as an anti-democratic force.

Interestingly, the Crick Report, which provided the basis for Citizenship in the National Curriculum for England, made no mention of racism when it presented the case for education for citizenship in the light of perceived threats to our democracy. Our analysis of the report (Osler, 2000) suggests that this important and in many ways valuable document may itself unwittingly reflect racism, particularly in its reference to minorities, who, it suggests, 'must learn and respect the laws, codes and conventions as much as the majority' (QCA, 1998: 17-18). No explanation is provided, but we are left with a number of possible interpretations, none of which is supported by evidence. One explanation is that the cultures and values of minorities are somehow at odds with the laws and conventions; another that minorities have not yet been socialised into these laws; and a third, that those drafting the report believe that individuals from minority communities are more likely to break the laws and conventions than are individuals from majority communities. One worrying feature is that minorities are lumped together as a homogeneous group and the same assumptions are made about all.

There are a number of other phrases and recommendations which give the Crick Report what is, in our judgement, a somewhat colonial flavour. In its discussion of national identity in a pluralist context, it refers to

> due regard being given to the homelands of *our* minority communities and to the main countries of British emigration. (QCA, 1998: 18, emphasis added)

Not only is it patronising in its use of the term 'our minority communities', but the assumption is made that members of minority communities (whether or not they are part of a migrant generation) will necessarily see the countries of their families' migration as their 'homelands' rather than Britain. It precludes the notion of multiple or hybrid identities and fails to recognise that individuals may have more than one 'homeland' and may identify themselves as *both* British *and* of a particular ethnic grouping. Indeed individuals may define themselves in a variety of ways, with emphasis being given to particular aspects in different contexts. So, for example, professional, family, linguistic and religious identities may be set alongside ethnic and national identities. An individual may see her or himself both Bangladeshi and British; as Miripuri, Muslim, Scottish and British; or as a teacher, British, Chinese and a Welsh speaker.

While issues of ethnicity are prominent in the report, these are not addressed in relation to inequality or differences in power. In fact there is no discussion of any ethnic differences in the participation rates or leadership roles of citizens. Race and racism, either institutional or interpersonal, receive no mention. Similarly there is no discussion of the different experiences of citizenship, or of leadership by women and men. On questions of gender the report is curiously silent.

From Crick to the Programmes of Study: racism introduced, human rights removed

The absence of reference to racism is remedied, to a degree, in the National Curriculum booklet for Citizenship at Key Stages 3 and 4 (DfEE/QCA, 1999a) and in the initial guidance for teachers. The former has a box on the cover which shows a few words from an anonymous piece of writing, apparently by a pupil. The one word that stands out is 'racism'. Thus the cover of the official publication makes a clear link between citizenship and racism. That said, there is little help provided for teachers wanting to explore the implications of this link. The initial guidance suggests that there should be 'consideration of local issues (such as particular manifestations of racism and its removal)' (QCA, 2000: 5), though no example is given of how schools might help to remove such local manifestations of racism. The guidance also recommends seven 'headings' for organising the study of citizenship and the first of these is 'human rights (including anti-racism)' (QCA, 2000: 20). Again, no example or further explanation is provided.

The Crick Report developed learning outcomes for Key Stage 3 (Years 7 to 9) and anticipated that young people would study the UN Convention on the Rights of the Child, the Universal Declaration of Human Rights and the European Convention on Human Rights. The context for this learning is expected to be concepts such as *discrimination, equal opportunities, tribunal, ballot, trade unions* for the UN Convention on the Rights of the Child and *prejudice, discrimination, xenophobia, pluralism* in the section mentioning the other two human rights instruments. Human rights as a concept is also linked to overseas aid, development and charity (QCA, 1998: 49-52).

The mention of specific human rights instruments disappears in the definitive programmes of study, to be replaced by a more general formulation: 'the legal and human rights and responsibilities underpinning society' (DfEE/QCA, 1999a:14). The initial guidance again provides no further elaboration or help for teachers.

A new multicultural vision

Modern Britain is often referred to as a multicultural society. Speaking to Muslim journalists, Prime Minister Tony Blair said:

> Today ...it is part of the accepted value system of Britain that we are multicultural and we are multiracial and that that is a strength, not a weakness. (*The Muslim News* 31 March 2000).

However, such affirmations are more likely to be made when addressing black and ethnic minority audiences than when addressing the largely white business community or the Women's Institute. Furthermore, in spite of the New Labour manifesto commitment, enacted by the introduction of the Race Relations Amendment Bill in 2000 to make racial harassment and racially motivated violence specific criminal offences, Government initiatives to promote this vision of a multicultural society have been less in evidence. Government policies, with some exceptions (Alibhai-Brown, 1999:7), tend to focus more broadly on reversing social exclusion, rather than directly addressing racial inequalities. So, for example, targets have been set to reduce the overall number of exclusions from school by one third by 2002 (Social Exclusion Unit, 1998). These targets fail to address the disproportionate numbers of exclusions from particular communities, notably African Caribbean boys and girls. The policy fails to consider the research evidence which suggests that when schools and LEAs are successful in cutting exclusions, they do so across the board, and that without specific targets and strategies for particular groups, such groups will remain disproportionately vulnerable to exclusion (Osler and Hill, 1999). It is also powerfully undermined by the enhanced power extended in Summer 2000 to headteachers to exclude pupils and the withdrawal of the right to appeal from parents and carers in many cases (*Times Educational Supplement,* 4 August 2000).

The term *multicultural* is widely used to refer to the fact that the processes of post-war immigration have led to the growth of visible minority communities. It is often used synonymously with ethnic minority or non-white, so that when schools are referred to as multicultural they are usually assumed to have high proportions of students of African Caribbean or Asian heritage. Some schools in predominantly white areas have adopted multicultural or antiracist policies with the explicit aim of challenging racist stereotyping and behaviour among their white pupils. Nevertheless, the concept of multiculturalism is often exclusive of white communities, which may mistakenly be assumed to be culturally homogeneous. Schools have a key role to play in the development of a new multicultural vision of Britain in the new century and in helping transform this vision into reality.

Identities, diversity and inequalities

Schools which pride themselves on celebrating the identities of black and other minority students' communities may fail to consider those of their white students. Moreover, they may focus on acknowledging and valuing cultural diversity without necessarily tackling structural inequality or directly challenging racism and discrimination. For instance, in a research project which examined how headteachers responded to assessments of race equality in school inspection, a headteacher reported how she was particularly supportive of minority students, encouraging them to organise celebrations in school and showing them how they were valued and respected, particularly since she recognised that some of her staff had 'a racist approach' (Osler and Morrison, 2000).

Antiracism is not an optional extra, however, but a responsibility of all. As a British Government minister stated in a parliamentary debate:

Anti-racism is not about helping black and Asian people; it is about our future – white and black. We all live in a multicultural society and we all have a choice: either we make a success of multicultural Britain or we do not. If we fail to address those issues, our children – white and black – will pay the price of that failure. That is why all of us, white and black, have a vested interest in the Bill and in anti-racism. We must make Britain a success as a multicultural society. (Mike O'Brien, Hansard 9 March 2000, column 1281)

Recent constitutional reform in the UK, including the establishment of a Scottish parliament and Welsh assembly, and the development of a new settlement between Britain and Northern Ireland, have led to increased interest and debate on what it means to be British and how citizenship is related to national and regional identities. So, for example, what does it mean to be British and Scottish? Meanings of nationality and national identity are being re-examined and re-defined. Citizenship does not depend solely on legal status; it also requires a sense of belonging. Consequently, within any programme of learning for citizenship, we will need to address the cultural and personal aspects of citizenship, focusing on issues of identity, as well as addressing structural and political issues (Osler and Starkey, 1996). Schools can – and should – play an important role in supporting and extending the identities of their students, enabling all of them, including white students, to feel a part of a multicultural society, and enabling all to participate in the future development of our democracy.

The diversity and range of identities within the white population is something that tends to be overlooked in a discourse of multiculturalism, and yet this population in Britain is far from homogenous. Within the education system there is now some recognition that it is important to think about the variety of ethnicities within the white population, (Troyna, 1998; Nayak, 1999). The Crick Report appears to support a recommendation that ' an explicit idea of multicultural citizenship needs to be formulated for Britain' (QCA, 1998:17; Policy Studies Institute, 1997). The political and constitutional developments in various parts of Britain and in Northern Ireland serve to illustrate how the process of identity development is an on-going project for individuals, influenced by political context as well as personal circumstance.

In the Crick Report the development of a common citizenship and a common national identity is seen as critical and it notes that 'matters of national identity in a pluralist society should never be taken for granted' (ibid., 1998: 18). This seems to imply a singular national identity, as if there were only one way of being British, or indeed English or Welsh. There may be elements of a national identity which all might share, but this core identity might be supplemented so that individuals might identify with the nation in a variety of ways. In the Crick Report and in much of the discourse on identities and citizenship there are far more references to 'difference', based on culture, religion, age, family, values, customs, economic, political and environmental circumstances, than to commonality or equality. Difference is portrayed as problematic, ignoring the reality that in any society there are likely to be tensions and that tensions can be creative and not necessarily destructive. Human rights provide a framework within which such tensions can be resolved peacefully, without resort to violence.

Human rights and political literacy

Although it sets out to make recommendations on citizenship education which will support the development of a healthy democracy, the Crick Report does not consider how citizenship education might support antiracism in education, and thus challenge a force which has the potential to undermine democracy and democratic citizenship. In Britain antiracism is often seen as simply the opposite of racism, rather than as a set of values or beliefs which are part of a broader human rights discourse (Lloyd, 1998; Bonnett, 2000). The report does place some emphasis on the teaching of human rights within the citizenship education programme. It also gives considerable weight to the concept of political literacy, which combines with social and moral responsibility and community involvement to form the three strands of the programme. Political literacy is defined as: 'pupils learning about and how to make themselves effective in public life through knowledge, skills and values' (QCA, 1998: 41).

Traditionally, multiculturalism in Britain has focused on the cultural and on issues of identity. In practice, many schools have avoided political and structural questions when dealing with the here and now. Such issues have often been reserved for history and geography lessons. Consequently, students' cultural development has often taken place in a political vacuum. The emphasis on political literacy in the Crick Report opens up a new opportunity to develop a more rounded curriculum, where questions of identity and cultural development are balanced with a knowledge and understanding of human rights and democratic practice (Osler and Starkey, 1996).

If we are to develop an inclusive concept of citizenship within a pluralist society and a form of citizenship education which genuinely supports and enables the development of democratic practice at all levels, we need to develop a new concept and vision of multiculturalism which is itself founded on human rights and is inclusive of all citizens, including majority white populations as well as minorities. This will require a recognition of the complex ways in which racism operates within Britain society, at both institutional and inter-personal levels. It will also require research and understanding of the ways in which individuals and groups have successfully challenged and overcome racism (Bonnett, 2000; Osler, 1997a). We need to acknowledge that racism and discrimination in British society are not confined to 'visible' and established minorities, but that other individuals and communities including refugees and asylum seekers, Jewish and Irish people, and Gypsies and Travellers may currently experience racism, prejudice, disadvantage, harassment and violence. A number of these communities may also recall a long history of racism and discrimination (Fryer, 1984).

A team that was examining the ways in which European Commission funded education and training projects contribute to active citizenship drew up a checklist designed for use by those planning citizenship education projects or curricula. In order to integrate the cognitive and affective elements, projects for citizenship require an appropriate pedagogy based on participation and active learning. An effective project is likely to include the following features:

- information about democracy and human rights in theory and in practice

- a focus on key skills for social and economic inclusion

- an equal opportunities dimension addressing the specific needs of women

- an antiracist focus and consideration of the specific needs of ethnic minorities

- opportunities to explore and reflect upon various identities and cultural attributes

- co-operative practice and group or team work

- experiential learning

- democratic decision-making, including participation in the management of the project

- independent reasoning and critical awareness

- development of effective communication skills including those required for transnational and intercultural communication

- community involvement

- negotiation and participation skills (Osler and Starkey, 1999).

This checklist might be adapted to serve the needs of those responsible for ensuring that their schools adequately prepare students for citizenship and for active participation in a democracy. It also provides us with a starting point for building upon the concept of political literacy as developed in the Crick Report. A politically literate citizen will require knowledge and understanding of human rights; opportunities to develop confident multiple identities; experience of democratic participation; and skills for social inclusion, for participation and to effect change.

Conclusion

A key aim of any programme of citizenship education must be the development of a society in which all citizens can claim their citizenship rights and responsibilities on the basis of equality.

Although the Crick Report recognises the importance of a common national identity and common citizenship, it assumes that visible ethnic minorities (and here it is referring to black British citizens, rather than white ethnicities such as Welsh or Scottish) need to change in order to realise this common citizenship. There is an implied process of assimilation or integration which requires more effort on the part of minorities than for white British citizens. Although the Government sees citizenship education as a key means of promoting racial equality through schooling, the concept of racism is absent from the Crick Report. Yet, with its emphasis on political literacy, the report does provide a key tool by which citizenship education programmes might be transformed to enable young people to confront and challenge racism. The challenge facing antiracist educators is to expand the concept of political literacy so that young people are not simply equipped with basic skills for participation but are also provided with knowledge and understanding of human rights as the principles underpinning democracy; are enabled to develop confident identities; and are equipped with the skills to challenge and confront inequality and effect change. Our citizenship education programmes will then have the potential to contribute to a new antiracist project which will strengthen democratic institutions and practices and enable the full participation of all.

References

Alibhai-Brown, Y. (1999) *True Colours: public attitudes to multiculturalism and the role of the government.* London: Institute of Public Policy Research.

Bonnett, A. (2000) *Anti-Racism.* London: Routledge.

Council of Europe (1985) Recommendation R (85) 7 of the Committee of Ministers to member States on Teaching and Learning about Human Rights in Schools, reprinted in: A. Osler and H. Starkey *Teacher Education and Human Rights.* London: David Fulton.

Council of Europe (1993) *Vienna Declaration*, 9 October. Strasbourg: Council of Europe.

Department for Education and Employment (1999) *DfEE News 272/99*, 16 June.

Department for Education and Employment /Qualifications and Curriculum Authority (1999a) *Citizenship: the National Curriculum for England. Key stages 3-4.* DfEE/QCA.

Department for Education and Employment/Qualifications and Curriculum Authority (1999b) *The National Curriculum: handbook for primary teachers in England.* DfEE/QCA.

Figueroa, P. (1999) Multiculturalism and anti-racism in a new ERA: a critical review. *Race Ethnicity and Education* 2 (2) 281-301.

Fryer, P. (1984) *Staying Power: the History of Black People in Britain*. London: Pluto.

Gillborn, D. and Gipps, C. (1996) *Recent Research on the Achievements of Ethnic Minority Pupils*. London: HMSO.

Holden, C. and Clough, N. (1998) (eds.) *Children as Citizens: education for participation in democracies old and new*. London: Jessica Kingsley.

Home Office (1999) *Stephen Lawrence Inquiry: Home Secretary's Action Plan*. London: Home Office.

Lloyd, C. (1998) *Discourses of Antiracism in France*. Aldershot: Ashgate.

Macpherson, W. *et al* (1999) *The Stephen Lawrence Inquiry*. London: The Stationery Office.

Nayak, A. (1999) 'White English Ethnicities': racism, anti-racism and student perspectives. *Race Ethnicity and Education* 2 (2) 177-202.

Osler, A. (1997a) *The Education and Careers of Black Teachers: changing identities, changing lives*. Buckingham: Open University Press.

Osler, A. (1997b) *Exclusion from School and Racial Equality: research report* London: Commission for Racial Equality.

Osler, A. (2000) The Crick Report: difference, equality and racial justice. *The Curriculum Journal,* 11 (1) 25-37.

Osler, A. and Hill, J. (1999) Exclusion from School: an examination of government proposals in the light of recent research evidence. *Cambridge Journal of Education,* 29 (1) 33-62.

Osler, A. and Morrison, M. (2000) *Inspecting Schools for Racial Equality: OFSTED's strengths and weaknesses. A report for the Commission for Racial Equality.* Stoke on Trent: Trentham.

Osler, A., Rathenow, H-F. and Starkey, H. (1996) (Eds.) *Teaching for Citizenship in Europe.* Stoke-on-Trent: Trentham.

Osler, A. and Starkey, H. (1996) *Teacher Education and Human Rights*. London: David Fulton.

Osler, A. and Starkey, H. (1999) Rights, identities and inclusion: European action programmes as political education *Oxford Review of Education,* 25 (1 and 2) 199-215.

Paxman, J. (1998) *The English: a portrait of a people*. London: Michael Joseph.

Policy Studies Institute (1997) *Ethnic Minorities in Britain: diversity and disadvantage (fourth national survey)*. London: PSI

Qualifications and Curriculum Authority (1998) *Education for Citizenship and the Teaching of Democracy in Schools*. Crick Report. London: QCA.

Qualifications and Curriculum Authority (2000) *Education for Citizenship: initial guidance for teachers*. London: QCA.

Ramsaran, C. (1999) An Intolerable Situation. *The Development Education Journal* 6 (1) 25-26.

Richardson, R. (1996) The terrestrial teacher, in: M. Steiner (ed.) *Developing the Global Teacher.* Stoke on Trent: Trentham.

Richardson, R. and Wood, A. (1999) *Inclusive Schools, Inclusive Society: race and identity on the agenda.* Stoke on Trent: Trentham.

Rothemund, A. (1995) *Domino: a manual to use peer group education as a means to fight racism, xenophobia, anti-Semitism and intolerance.* Strasbourg: Council of Europe.

Social Exclusion Unit (1998) *Truancy and School Exclusion.* London: Cabinet Office.

Starkey, H. (2000) Citizenship education in France and Britain: evolving theories and practices. *Curriculum Journal*, 11 (1) 39-54.

Troyna, B. (1998) 'The whites of my eyes, nose, ears...': a reflexive account of 'whiteness' in race-related research, in: P.Connolly and B.Troyna (eds.) *Researching Racism in Education: politics, theory and practice.* Buckingham: Open University Press.

2

The Implications of the Human Rights Act for Citizenship Education

Sarah Spencer

W hen the Human Rights Act came into force on 2 October 2000, its ostensible aim was to ensure that Government and public authorities across the UK act in a way that is compatible with the European Convention on Human Rights. If they fail to do so, individuals can now challenge the authority in court. But extending the statutory responsibilities of public bodies, and the legal rights of individuals, was only ever one part of what the Government was setting out to achieve. Its goal was much bolder: to develop a culture of respect for human rights within public bodies and among the public at large. Moreover, the Task Force set up by the Home Secretary to advise the Government on implementation of the Act was given the task of raising awareness of the importance of human rights principles, 'especially among young people'.

The rights in the European Convention have been binding on the UK Government and public authorities since the Convention came into force in 1953. The difficulty has been only that of enforcing those rights, with a procedure that required individuals to seek a remedy in the European Court of Human Rights in Strasbourg. Taking up to five years for a case to receive a final judgement, this was a path only for the most dogged and determined. Moreover, the limited enforceability of the rights gave public authorities little incentive to prioritise compliance.

Some of the cases which reached the Strasbourg Court have nevertheless been of enormous importance, not least that which led to the final abolition of birching and the case which led to the end of corporal punishment in schools. But no one could say that the standards in the Convention have, until now, been an ever present concern to those running the plethora of public bodies up and down the country. The Human Rights Act will change that.

The Act incorporates the rights in the Convention into UK law so that they are enforceable in all of our courts and tribunals. Individuals who believe that they have been subject to religious intolerance or degrading treatment, for instance, who have been prevented from speaking publicly about an issue of concern or, indeed, denied the right to education, will be able to seek a remedy, without delay, in our own domestic courts. The intention is that public authorities should review their practices to ensure that they do not unwittingly infringe the Convention, and many authorities undertook extensive preparation before the Act came into force (although, regrettably, many did not). The definition of public authority under the Act, incidentally, includes any body which fulfils a 'public function'. It thus embraces local education authorities and schools, including those in the private sector.

The Act itself is thus largely to do with providing legal remedies when things go wrong. But the Government has said that it wants the legislation to have a far wider impact, to create, as the Home Secretary has said, a 'culture of rights'. Within public bodies, the Act will indeed make human rights principles 'all-pervasive' by requiring staff to consider, when exercising their discretion, whether their actions (or inaction) could infringe someone's human rights. If so, they must consider whether their action is proportionate to the goal they are trying to achieve. As the Home Secretary puts it:

> Ministers and public authorities will need to be ready to show that they have had Convention principles constantly in mind in making decisions affecting people's civil and political rights. In time, the language of the Convention will be the language in which many of the key debates are

settled; the language you need to speak to win an argument. And that's a real culture change. (Straw, 1999)

While the primary focus is on achieving culture change within public bodies, the Government has made clear its wider goal of achieving greater respect for human rights within the population as a whole. The potential to raise such awareness among young people was emphasised during the passage of the Bill through Parliament by Baroness Williams, a former Secretary of State for Education. In the context of a debate on the need for a Human Rights Commission to promote and enforce the Act, she argued that the Commission

> ...would, I hope, become the spark for a new attempt in our education system to introduce the concept of citizenship alongside that of religion and ethics. I can think of nothing more appropriate at the beginning of a new government than to accept the need for a culture of human rights among our children and university and college students, because this is the bedrock upon which a culture of human rights will be built in this country. (Baroness Williams, House of Lords, 3 November 1997: Column 1301)

The Crick Report

The creation of a human rights culture, and its implications for young people, were not, however, part of the thinking behind the establishment of the Advisory Group for the Teaching of Citizenship and Democracy in English schools. Established in November 1997, only a month after publication of the Human Rights Bill, its role was to provide a statement of the aims and purposes of citizenship education in schools and a broad framework for what that component of the curriculum might look like. The relevance of human rights principles to citizenship education was nevertheless not mentioned in the terms of reference for the group. No connection appears to have been made, at that stage, between this initiative from the Department for Education and Employment (DfEE) and the human rights agenda developing only a few hundred metres down the road in the Home Office.

There was a great deal in the Advisory Group's interim report, in March 1998, that was welcome. It did, however, disappoint those concerned to see the development of human rights education, by failing to mention any role that it might play. To his credit, the Chair of the group, Professor Crick, engaged with his critics and the final report (QCA, 1998) reflected that subsequent dialogue. In so doing, it began to bridge the gap between the DfEE's concern to promote education for citizenship and the Home Office's concern to foster respect for human rights and the responsibilities they entail.

The final report of the Advisory Group thus took a different approach. It included human rights instruments and issues among those which pupils should be expected to know and understand; concepts such as equality, diversity, human rights and responsibilities amongst those which children should discuss; a belief in human dignity and equality, a commitment to equal opportunities and a concern for human rights among the values which citizenship education should be expected to promote; and an ability to tolerate the views of others among the essential human rights skills which pupils might be expected to learn.

The Crick Report was considered by the Qualifications and Curriculum Authority and the DfEE, and its recommendations were effectively implemented by the Order which officially introduced Citizenship into the curriculum and the programmes of study for secondary schools (DfEE/QCA, 1999a) and non-statutory guidelines for primary schools (DfEE/QCA, 1996b) which followed. Human rights issues and principles found a place among the many issues, concepts and skills to be learnt. But there remains a sense in which human rights is included as an option, rather than at the heart of the skills and values which young people need to learn. This is not to say that citizenship education should not embrace far broader concerns than human rights. It should. But I shall argue that human rights principles are the essence of social and moral responsibility, and thus should lie at the heart of citizenship education, not be peripheral to it.

Social and moral responsibility

The Crick Report rightly said that children need to be taught moral values – but whose? The subsequent guidance to schools leaves open which source of values they should use, pointing to lists of values drawn up by Crick and by the earlier Forum on Values in Education in the Community, while suggesting that for some the source should be the religious beliefs on which the school was founded. There is, however, a strong case for saying that the values which schools promote ought to be ones that have wide acceptance and a legitimacy deriving from a higher source of authority than a government advisory body, or a single religion. Moreover, they should contribute to developing a core minimum of common values on which a consensus can be built across a culturally diverse society.

International human rights standards provide that framework of values. They have an authority beyond any code of ethics agreed at national level and, being a balanced package of rights and responsibilities, entirely fit the objectives of education for citizenship. The European Convention, in particular, provides an ethical framework to teach children the elements of social responsibility needed to function successfully both in the school environment and later as adults.

If one examines the content of the European Convention it is clear that respect for the rights of others lies at its heart. It teaches us to ensure that everyone is given a fair hearing (Article 6); to listen to the views of others even when we disagree (Article 10); to respect each other's privacy (Article 8) and someone's religious beliefs even if they are very different from our own (Article 9). It stresses the value of peaceful protest (Article 11); provides that there should be an effective remedy for people who think that their rights have been denied (Article 13); and teaches us that we must not treat people in a degrading way (Article 3). It reminds us that anyone charged with an offence should be presumed innocent until proved guilty (Articles 5 and 6) and that no one should be subject to unfair discrimination (Article 14). The Convention teaches that everyone is entitled to the peaceful enjoyment of their own possessions; guarantees a right to education; and ensures that people can freely express their choice of representatives at the ballot box (Protocol 1).

No right answer

These rights are not, however, absolute. With rare exceptions (such as freedom from torture), all of them can be restricted in certain circumstances. That may be to protect public safety, to prevent crime and disorder or to protect health, or to protect the rights and freedoms of others. The Convention does not, therefore, provide absolute rights nor absolute answers. What it does do is provide a framework in which a conflict of interests, a moral dilemma, can be discussed; a framework which avoids the danger of moral relativism without imposing 'right' or 'wrong' answers.

Recognising that, one of the teaching approaches used in Canada, for instance, is to introduce pupils to real human rights cases that have come before the courts. The pupils are given the circumstances of the case but debate the issues without knowing the judgement reached by the court. When they discuss the merits of the case they can use the provisions of Canada's Charter of Rights to support their case for, or against, the individual concerned. It could be the right, for instance, of a Sikh boy to carry his ceremonial dagger to school, versus the school rule, on grounds of safety, that no weapons of any kind be brought onto the premises.

Finally, the pupils learn the judgement that the court came to and its reasons for doing so. Drawing on human rights instruments in such debates does not impose solutions. They usually provide only a moral and legal framework, a benchmark of minimum standards, within which to discuss the merits of the case.

Rights and responsibilities in balance

There is sometimes a fear that teaching young people about human rights will fill them with assertive confidence about their own rights while ignoring the responsibilities they also have to respect the rights of others. The concern is that they may adopt the bolshy 'I know my rights' line that parents and teachers dread!

There is indeed a place for providing children with the facts about their rights under the law. They need to know, for instance, at what age they are allowed to buy cigarettes or alcohol if we expect them to obey the law. And, for their own safety, they need to know what it is lawful for adults to do to them, and what to do if they think that their rights have been infringed. But to teach legal rights in a vacuum would be a travesty of what human rights education should be about. Human rights are not about individuals in isolation but a system for ensuring respect for mutual responsibilities. My neighbour's right to privacy imposes an obligation on me to respect it. The individual's freedom from discrimination is the employer's obligation to prevent such treatment. Teaching human rights means teaching responsibilities as well (see Osler and Starkey, this volume, chapter 7).

Common values

The ethical framework provided by international human rights standards is particularly important in a multicultural country in which we need a basic set of common values which amount to more than the majority imposing their values on minorities. For that reason, the Home Secretary has rightly argued that a human rights culture, fostered by the Human Rights Act, will be a unifying force in our diverse, multicultural society:

> Consider the nature of modern British society. It's a society enriched by different cultures and faiths. It needs a formal shared understanding of what is fundamentally right and fundamentally wrong if it is to work together in unity and confidence...
>
> The Human Rights Act provides that formal shared understanding. It's an ethical language we can all recognise and sign up to. An ethical language which doesn't belong to any particular group or creed but to all of us. One that is based on principles of our common humanity. (Straw, 1999)

A successful multicultural society achieves an optimal balance between unity and diversity. Common values draw us together, but they also need to facilitate our understanding, and negotiation, of difference. Human rights standards provide that framework.

Dull charters and legal language?

Understanding that teaching about human rights means teaching about the responsibilities they entail should help to overcome some of the resistance to teaching this subject in schools. Realising that it does not mean teaching right and wrong answers to complex moral dilemmas, but provides a framework of values in which they can be negotiated, is equally important. But there are further grounds for resistance. Many believe, for instance, that teaching about human rights means learning the contents of international charters of rights, and necessitates using legalistic concepts and language to which children cannot relate.

We know from experience, however, that even very young pupils understand notions of fairness, of privacy, of a right to have one's side of the incident heard, and of a punishment that is out of proportion to the offence. The fact that they would struggle with the language used in court to discuss those issues does not mean that they cannot be discussed at all. If human rights are taught so that they relate to the pupils' own life experiences and delivered in an entertaining, participative way, they can be stimulating and enjoyable.

Very young children in Canada, for instance, have been taught about law and punishment by putting the character from a well known children's story, Goldilocks, on trial. When she entered the bears' home and ate their porridge, what was she doing that was wrong? Were there any grounds to excuse her behaviour and, if not, what should her punishment be? Who should decide?

Older pupils in South Africa have discussed the case of three ship-wrecked sailors, loosely based on a real-life English case from the last century. The pupils are given a picture showing three men in a boat, 1600 kilometres from land, 25 days after their ship sank. They have no food or water. The caption says:

> Bob, Dan and Sam agreed that one of them should be killed and eaten by the other two. But when it turned out to be him, Bob wasn't so keen any more.

Five days later, Dan and Sam are rescued by a passing ship and brought to land. Pupils are told that the law says that any person who intentionally and unlawfully kills another is guilty of murder. It then asks them:

- Should Dan and Sam be charged with murder?

- If you were their lawyer, what arguments would you make?

- If they are found guilty, what should their punishment be?

- What would be the purpose of convicting them?

- What is the connection between law and morality in this case – was it morally wrong for Dan and Sam to kill Bob?

- Can it be morally right but unlawful? (McQuoid, 1987).

In a lesson of that kind there is great scope for teaching about the law, how the courts work, about punishment and its purpose, as well as about moral dilemmas, that there are not always right and wrong answers, and that people may legitimately differ in the conclusion they reach. Each of those is an important lesson for life.

South Africa provides a further example of an exercise in which young people can learn about law and about conflicts between fundamental rights, while developing practical skills. The University of the Western Cape runs mock trial competitions for secondary schools. During 1999 the case – in which schools had to choose whether to represent the prosecution or the defence – concerned a six year old child with AIDS. His parents were deeply religious and refused to allow him to have medical treatment. An aunt called an ambulance but the parents turned it away. The child died and the parents were charged with murder. Were they guilty, or were they exercising their freedom of religion? The pupils had to argue the case. This is a lesson on the law, on criminal procedure, but also on conflicting rights.

Learning by experience

The Crick Report argued that children cannot simply be taught how to be effective citizens, they need to learn by experience. Within school, and in the outside community, young people need to learn the skills of persuasion, of conflict resolution, of decision-making. While the logic of that argument cannot be down-said, its impact could be greater than the introduction of the citizenship curriculum itself.

If, for instance, we want children to have the confidence to express their views and to respect the views of others – one of the objectives of citizenship education – schools will need to create an environment in which they can acquire that confidence. Throughout the day, in the classroom and outside, young people will need to be in an environment in which they can express opinions, knowing that they will not be ridiculed by their teacher or classmates. For pupils to learn by experience in this way – through participation in decision making in a constructive, accepting environment – would require a significant change of ethos in many schools.

The UN Committee which monitors the Convention on the Rights of the Child has repeatedly recommended that governments take steps to encourage greater participation by children at schools. The Convention requires that as children develop the ability to take decisions for themselves, they should be encouraged to do so.

A former Director-General of UNESCO put it this way:

> Education for human rights and democracy in the last analysis means the empowerment of each and every individual to participate with an active sense of responsibility in all aspects of political and social life.....
>
> the entire school system should constitute an initiation to democratic living – to the assumption of responsibilities, to the challenges of participation, to learning about the linkage between rights and duties, knowing and caring. (Mayor, 1993)

Again, we ought not to think of this approach as the prerogative of secondary schools.

At Highfield Junior School in Plymouth, as in many other primary schools, teachers and pupils use circle time to make decisions about rules in the classroom and to sort out problems (see Alderson, this volume). They start by reminding themselves of the rules governing their discussion:

- only talk one at a time
- be kind and don't say anything that will hurt somebody
- listen carefully
- talk clearly so that everyone can hear you.

The Headteacher of the school says of this model:

> Everyone learns that what they have to say is valid, valuable and valued by the others in the class or group – even if their wish is simply to say 'pass'.

Children were learning that they had the right to have a say – but not the right to be right. (Highfield School, 1997)

Research by Osler (2000) has shown that pupil participation in school decision making, and in particular in making decisions on rules and discipline, can increase the effectiveness of behaviour management. The recent Eurodem project, which reviewed pupil democracy in Europe, concluded that where children have been given a voice:

relationships in schools were predominantly human, equitable, warm and non-confrontational. Pupils felt they could give their opinions and that teachers listened to them. Pupils interviewed showed confidence and high levels of articulation...There appeared to be far fewer problems in school with discipline, even in schools located in very deprived social areas, and there was equally far less concern over the issue of school exclusions than is the case in the UK. (Davies and Kirkpatrick, 2000)

The Government has accepted the value of pupil participation and the proposed attainment target in the citizenship curriculum for pupils of 14 years states that they must participate in school and community based activities. At 16 years they must also demonstrate a willingness to evaluate such activity critically, and demonstrate responsibility to others and their local communities.

South Africa also provides some positive examples of participation at school and in the wider community. In Voorspoed primary school in Cape Town, for instance, which is situated in a deprived, mixed-race township, children are first of all taught conflict resolution as a standard part of the curriculum, to enable them to deal with the tensions they bring to school (see also Harber, this volume). Children of all ages are taught to recognise the sources of conflict in their own life, how to deal with their anger, to generate options for resolving conflict and how to beg to differ.

Some of the 12 year old children who have completed the course can then choose to train as mediators, an eight hour course after school. 'I used to judge people. Now I listen. There are two sides to every story', one 12 year old told me when I visited the school. Her friend said: 'I fight less with other children now. I feel calmer'. The headteacher says:

often it is the pupils who have been most disruptive in the past who volunteer and they are surprisingly good at it... and we invariably find that the mediators' school work improves. Finding that they can help others enhances their self- esteem and that has all kinds of benefits.

The techniques that Voorspoed pioneered are now being introduced in over 100 schools in the Cape, ahead of the formal introduction of 'life orientation' and education for democracy in South Africa's curriculum 2005.

Human Rights Commission

The case for human rights education in England has been accepted. It will form one element of the secondary school Citizenship curriculum from 2001. But the extent to which schools do in practice build human rights into the curriculum that is taught, and create a rights and responsibilities ethos in the school, remains very much an open question. The DfEE is unlikely to encourage schools to pay more than cursory attention to this aspect of the curriculum and it is not within the remit of the Home Office. If human rights education is to become the experience of every pupil, what will be the engine to drive it?

In countries with Human Rights Commissions, as in much of the Commonwealth, there is a body with the expertise, and sometimes the resources, to work with the curricular authorities to ensure that appropriate material is available. The Indian Human Rights Commission, for instance, has placed great emphasis on this aspect of its work, as has the new Commission in South Africa (Spencer and Bynoe, 1998). The Northern Ireland Human Rights Commission, established in 1999, has an education worker who has responsibility for promoting human rights education, working with the education authorities. In June 2000 the Scottish Executive announced its intention to publish consultation proposals for a Scottish Human Rights Commission, which would undoubtedly have a responsibility to promote awareness of the importance of human rights values. Only in England and Wales is there no move, as yet, to establish such a body, although there may be an inquiry on the issue during 2001 by the newly established Joint Parliamentary Select Committee on Human Rights.

Conclusion

The first aim of the Human Rights Act is to require Government and public authorities to comply with the European Convention on Human Rights, and to enable individuals to seek a remedy in our domestic courts if they fail to do so. But the Government's objective is that the Act should create a culture of respect for human rights within public bodies, and among the public at large – particularly among young people. No connection was initially made with the DfEE's initiative to develop citizenship education, but human rights did find a place in the Order introducing that new element of the curriculum and in the guidance to schools which followed. Nevertheless, the extent to which pupils will in practice be exposed to human rights knowledge, values and skills, and the responsibilities which human rights principles entail, remains uncertain.

I argued that human rights principles are central to social and moral responsibility and should therefore lie at the heart of citizenship education. Requiring respect for the rights of others, these principles are a balanced framework of rights and responsibilities, relevant to life within the school and in the community as adults. Teaching human rights means exposing young people to this framework of values, within which they can discuss real situations in which rights conflict. Lessons can be relevant and stimulating, even for the very young. There is also scope to learn by experience, through participation in decision-making, and through learning the skills of conflict resolution. There is evidence that such teaching practices improves relationships in schools and reduces behavioural problems.

Finally, for human rights education to find its place within the citizenship curriculum in primary and secondary schools, there may need to be a driver for change. This role could be fulfilled by a statutory body, a Human Rights Commission, as in many Commonwealth countries and in Northern Ireland. For such a body, fostering a culture of respect for the human rights of others among the adults of the future would be its greatest challenge.

References

Alderson, P. (2000) Practising democracy in two inner city schools, in: A. Osler (ed.) *Citizenship and Democracy in Schools: diversity, identity, equality*. Stoke on Trent: Trentham.

Davies, L. and Kirkpatrick, G. (2000) *The Eurodem project, a review of pupil democracy in schools*. Childrens' Rights Alliance.

Department for Education and Employment/Qualifications and Curriculum Authority (1999a) *Citizenship: the National Curriculum for England*. Key stages 3-4. DfEE/QCA.

Department for Education and Employment/Qualifications and Curriculum Authority (1999b) *The National Curriculum: handbook for primary teachers in England*. DfEE/QCA.

Harber, C. (2000) Schools, democracy and violence in South Africa, in: A. Osler (ed.) *Citizenship and Democracy in Schools: diversity, identity, equality*. Stoke on Trent: Trentham.

Highfield School (ed. P Alderson) (1997) *Changing Our School: promoting positive behaviour.* London: Institute of Education/Plymouth: Highfield School.

McQuoid D (1987) *Street Law, Practical Law for South African students*, Book 1, Association of Law Societies of South Africa.

Mayor, F. (1993) *Opening Address to the International Congress on Education for Human Rights and Democracy*. Montreal, Canada, 8 March. Paris: UNESCO.

Osler, A. (2000) Children's rights, responsibilities and understandings of school discipline, *Research Papers in Education*, 15(1) 49-67.

Osler, A. and Starkey, H. (2000) Human rights, responsibilities and school self-evaluation in: A. Osler (ed.) *Citizenship and Democracy in Schools: diversity, identity, equality*. Stoke on Trent: Trentham.

Qualifications and Curriculum Authority (1998) *Education for Citizenship and the Teaching of Democracy in Schools*, QCA/98/155.

Spencer, S. and Bynoe, I. (1998) *A Human Rights Commission, the Options for Britain and Northern Ireland*, Institute for Public Policy Research.

Straw, J. (1999) *Building a Human Rights Culture*. The Home Secretary's address to Civil Service College Seminar, 9 December.

3

Children's Rights and Education

Eugeen Verhellen

hildren's rights in education need to be seen as inclusive and comprehensive so it is important that they be addressed in the context of a basic legislative framework, namely the Convention on the Rights of the Child. By adopting this framework we are able to address fundamental questions about expectations and demands on the various actors in the school culture, particularly teachers and students. We are also able to avoid solutions which rely on mere rhetoric or on temporary technical fixes. This chapter considers how children's rights might be implemented in schools and addresses both attitudinal changes and strategies.

Changing constructs of the child and human rights

For very important historical reasons children tend to be seen as future performers in a yet-to-be-created splendid Enlightened Society. This social construct of childhood, which defines it as a stage of preparation for adult life, had and continues to have enormous consequences for children and for those who relate to them. For children themselves it means that they are seen as not-yets: children are defined as not yet knowing, not yet competent, and not yet being. By defining childhood as a preparation or transition period, children are placed in a state of limbo. They are obliged to wait and are required to prepare themselves as future performers.

In recent decades this adult-centric construct of the child has been questioned. New understandings of childhood and changing perceptions of children have led to children's right to enjoy their rights in the here and now being widely advocated. Thus children are recognised as individuals entitled to human dignity. Respect for children as human beings means that they are no longer perceived as mere *objects* of protection but as *subjects*, bearers of human rights like all human beings. This new perception applies to the child as an individual as well as to children as a social category. This raises implications for both psychologists and sociologists of education.

This conceptual switch in the construct of the child is not easy to implement and practise in daily life. It requires a complete revision of approach, since we are not used to treating children from a human rights standpoint. The UN Convention on the Rights of the Child (CRC) strongly promotes this human rights approach.

The Convention on the Rights of the Child
Comprehensive

The preamble of the CRC, which does not present binding principles, nevertheless outlines the terms of reference within which we should interpret the various binding articles which follow. The preamble stresses that the CRC is an integral part of the human rights project.

The Convention itself contains both civil and political and social, economic and cultural rights. It effectively reminds us that these rights are, in fact, inseparable. All rights are equally important and interdependent. No right can stand on its own. This would be in contravention of the spirit of the CRC.

This requires governments, lawyers and other experts to take a novel approach since they are used to reading and interpreting Conventions article by article. In other words the CRC demands a comprehensive and interactive interpretation, thus setting a standard for future human rights instruments and for the human rights project as a whole. The process of transforming children's rights standards into reality may act as a catalyst for future democratic development.

For heuristic reasons only and keeping in mind the indivisibility of rights, it is useful to divide the CRC into categories or subdivisions. So, for example, it is helpful to consider the 3 Ps: provision, protection and participation rights (Helio *et al*, 1993).

Protection rights exist because of children's vulnerability and dependence. Children have the right to be protected from those with greater power. Such rights include the right to life, survival and development (Article 6), and the right to protection from abuse, neglect and exploitation (Article19). The basic idea behind protection rights is that children have the right to be protected, to be shielded from individual and structural harmful acts and practices. The right of access to provisions include information (Article17), social security (Article 26), the highest level of health (Article 24), and education (Article 29).

The most revolutionary part of the CRC is found among the articles addressing *participation* rights. These recognise the right of children to make certain choices for themselves and present them in dialogue with others. Such rights include the right to express an opinion, freedom of thought, conscience and religion, freedom of association, protection of privacy (Articles 12-16). These participation rights recognise children as meaning-makers and acknowledge their citizenship.

Legally binding

The CRC is a Convention, which means that State Parties ratifying it accept the legal obligation to implement the provisions of the Convention (*Pacta sunt servanda-principle*).

At the domestic level, State Parties that adopt the Constitutional provision of the so-called 'self-executing force' are bound via their courts to apply this strong provision to the CRC. Hesitations in this regard can cause weakening of the CRC since amending laws is not always a guarantee that they are strengthened. Countries that have a dualistic system have to transpose the CRC into national laws.

At the international level there is a Committee on the Rights of the Child (Article 43) which monitors all State Parties' compliance via a system of initial and periodic reports (Article 44) from these States. State Parties are required to make their reports and the observations of the Committee widely available to the public in their countries (Article 44.6). This provision in its turn is a consequence of Article 42, which obliges State Parties to make the rights contained in the CRC widely known to both adults and children (Verhellen, 1996).

The over-riding importance of this binding duty, both to report and inform, clearly strengthens the legal power of the Convention. The implementation of the Convention is thus a sustainable process.

Universal ratification

In itself, and as part of the international human rights project, the CRC has quite a long history. On 20 November 1989, after ten years of preparation, the General Assembly of the UN adopted without a dissenting vote, the Convention on the Rights of the Child. The CRC contains 54 articles of which 41 are substantive articles defining the rights of the child and the obligations on State Parties ratifying the Convention. Unlike the two former instruments which address children's rights, the CRC is a Convention and is thus legally binding.

Within a year the UN had secured 20 signatories for the Convention, the minimum number needed to enable its entry into force. The Convention entered into force on 2 September 1990. This speedy and massive response of the international community to the Convention is unique in the history of human rights. To date 191 States have ratified the CRC. The only exceptions are Somalia and the USA. The realisation of almost universal ratification is a unique milestone in the history of human rights. By its comprehensiveness, by its binding character, and by its universal ratification, the CRC is now challenging the world with a new geo-political social contract.

However, this very important phase of standard setting is only a first stage. Implementation and monitoring are urgently required. This will not occur automatically. Since the CRC is a Convention and so legally binding, children have the right to legal protection of their rights. Legal protection of children's rights is more than just a judicial process.

Legal protection of children's rights

The CRC irrevocably closed the era of children's protection and opened a new era of the legal protection of the *rights* of children. In other words, in legal terms, it underlined the evolution of the child as a legal *object* into the child as a legal *subject*.

The legal protection of rights implies more than just judicial procedures. It has to comply with simple but basic requirements. To mention some:

- You must *have* rights

- You must be *informed* about your rights

- You must be able to *exercise* your rights

- If necessary you must be able to *enforce* your rights

- There must be a community of interest to *advocate* your rights. (Verhellen, 1995)

Each of these requirements is *interdependent*. If one of them is not met or is inadequately met, legal protection is seriously jeopardised. Just as the construct of the child is undergoing processes of deconstruction and reconstruction, so such requirements are not self-evident in discussions of legal protection of children's rights.

Human rights education policy: supporting children's rights

Education cannot be restricted only to the area of schooling. It covers a broad scope of activities in a far wider field of application (see, for example: UNCHR, 1995; Tarrow, 1992; Lynch, 1992; Brock-Utne, 1994; Richardson, 1991). Articles 17 and 42 of the CRC are clear in this regard. Nevertheless, a large part of learning takes place in the organised school education system. As a consequence education within the school system plays a key role in human rights education policy, which in turn supports children's rights. Among the interrelated requirements for an effective legal protection of rights, human rights education is particularly important. In itself it is embedded in a much wider relationship between children's rights and education.

Children's rights within the school system

Children spend a considerable part of their existence at school. School, as an instrument of socialisation, is expected to reflect developments in society. The global social development of new constructs of the child creates new needs. Education has to take these new developments into account or, at the very least, to be aware of them. In ideal circumstances, education can even provide the stimulus to such developments. Developments in the concept of human rights go a long way towards explaining why the law is now a hot topic in education. Surveys, and an increasing number of court rulings, show that in many countries pupils are going to court to resolve disputes arising at school. This is a remarkable development, given that in the past education, traditionally based on the absolute power of teachers, remained untouched by the law. A century ago, it would have been unthinkable for a pupil to appeal against the decision of a headteacher.

Although, because of the nature of the rights it confers, the CRC in many cases imposes obligations on State Parties, it also grants a number of general human rights to children. This new impetus to children's self-determination cannot but produce new, important tasks for education. Describing the relationship between education and the rights of the child is not easy. It is a relationship with many facets and problems, not always immediately obvious. When a State ratifies the CRC, the implementation carries serious consequences for the school system. Through ratification three important tasks are imposed on schools: namely, the right to education; rights in education; and rights through education (Verhellen, 1993). These tasks have implications for the school culture or ethos.

The right to education

In various national and international legal instruments, the right to education is recognised as a universal fundamental right in society. The right to education is covered by Article 26 of the Universal Declaration on Human Rights (1948), which, however, is not binding. It was later repeatedly confirmed in binding international legal instruments. Article 13 of the International Covenant on Economic,

Social and Cultural Rights, adopted by the UN in 1966, imposes an obligation on State Parties to recognise the 'right of every person to education'. In its articles 4 and 5, the UNESCO Convention (1960) develops this right still further and deals more particularly with the principle of non-discrimination in education. Article 2 of the first Additional Protocol (1952) to the European Convention on Human Rights also reaffirms this right by stating: 'No person shall be denied the right to education'.

The CRC obviously also reconfirms this right. Article 28 provides the means of enforcing it. The principle of non-discrimination, the right of free access to education, and the introduction of compulsory primary education are examples of subjects covered by this right to education. Article 29 contains detailed provisions concerning the aims and values involved: the development of the child's personality to its fullest potential; the preparation of the child for a responsible role in society; the development of respect for nature; mutual understanding and friendship among all peoples; and especially the development of respect for human rights and fundamental freedoms. Both articles therefore impose the obligation on States Parties to implement the Convention *directly* through their education policy. At first sight, most Western industrialised countries do seem to live up to the obligations imposed by the above mentioned international instruments. And yet a considerable number of problems to do with this right to education have arisen. The number of court cases at domestic and international (European) level is on the increase. It is impossible to deal with all these problem areas in the confines of this chapter but some examples will illustrate their complexity.

First of all, much doubt has been expressed about the concept of 'every person', which can be regarded either as a negative reference to the principle of non-discrimination, or as a positive reference to the democratisation role which education can play. Various studies have demonstrated the existence of inequality of educational opportunity for certain categories of people. Access to education may be free, but that is not the end of it. Free access means there are no school fees, but it does not mean there are no other (sometimes quite substantial) expenses for all kinds of compulsory or optional activities. These extra costs may well indirectly cause problems for certain people in asserting their right to education. Recent surveys have demonstrated that democratisation in education is stagnating. The proportion of children from the so-called lower social classes in higher education and at university is extremely low.

Phenomena such as dropping out, truancy, unsuitable curricula, all have to do with the content and formal quality of education. This is directly connected to the real aim of education, which may be regarded as in many ways in conflict with Article 29 of the Convention – that is to say, with the development of the child's personality, talents and mental and physical abilities to their fullest potential. Expelling children subject to compulsory schooling (see Blair, this volume) or refusing to enrol them is also a focus of highly topical debate. These are incidents which occur regularly and have far-reaching consequences for children, who cannot fight these decisions. The growing number of court cases involving students and the education authorities clearly demonstrates that the former have had little protection until now.

Rights in education
The right to education as a fundamental human right has to be guaranteed directly. However, the rights enshrined in the CRC must be implemented by the school system in indirect ways. In other words, one of the first tasks for State Parties is to clarify children's legal position in education and to prevent breaches of children's rights. For example, attention needs to be given to such issues as disciplinary rules and procedures.

In its articles 12 to 16 the CRC contains important fundamental freedoms: the right to express an opinion; freedom of expression; freedom of thought, conscience and religion; freedom of association; protection of privacy. This clearly implies the introduction of rights to self-determination which must also be implemented in the daily school culture. It implies human rights *in* education. Far too little thinking has been done on this matter. Effectively little attention has been given to ensuring that children are guaranteed respect in schools. To illustrate this statement consider Article12.2 (CRC):

For this purpose (i.e. to implement the right to freedom of opinion and to freedom of expression), the child shall in particular be provided the opportunity to be heard in any judicial and administrative proceedings affecting the child.

This is a clear reference to the need for participation in daily school life.

Rights through education

The UNESCO-Convention (1960 – Article 5) and the International Covenant on Economic, Social and Cultural Rights (1966 – Article 13) clearly indicate that State Parties must aim at promoting respect for human rights through education. This is also in line with the spirit of the UN Charter and the Universal Declaration of Human Rights (Article 26.2), in that familiarity with human rights is the best protection against infringements.

The Council of Europe Committee of Ministers has also adopted a recommendation (Recommendation R(85)7) in which it urges Member States to give firm encouragement to education in human rights and its promotion. It asks Member States to draw its recommendation to the attention of everybody involved in education. The recommendation contains a large number of detailed suggestions to this end. The Parliamentary Assembly of the Council of Europe later reaffirmed the need for human rights education by adopting its recommendation 1346 (26 September 1997). Such initiatives are re-affirmed by the UN Decade for Human Rights Education 1995–2004.

It is not surprising that we should encounter the same idea in the CRC (Article 29.1.b). The Convention goes one step further. Article 42 imposes the obligation on State Parties to make the principles and provisions of the Convention widely known to adults and children alike. Moreover, Article 44.6 requests State Parties to make the periodic reports and the comments from the Committee widely available to the public in their own countries. A permanent, large scale information campaign on the Convention and its content is obviously essential if it is to be implemented effectively.

It is equally obvious that education has a major responsibility in this respect. Spending an occasional hour or two on the subject of children's rights in schools would clearly fall short of the obligations State Parties have taken upon themselves. Essentially, there has to be a shift in fundamental attitudes on respect for children's rights. Theoretical teaching on the values of human rights and democracy serves little purpose if these values are not also put into practice.

Apart from this shift in attitudes, we will need changes in existing school curricula. Respect for human rights can be taught not only in history lessons but through practically every subject. Teacher training will have to be adapted to this new task. There might also be specific training for (regional) press and information officers and the setting up of a specific information system. Finally, all kinds of educational aids could be designed, for example, texts, audio-visual aids, educational games and exhibitions.

Expectations and Demands

It is clear that the human rights project and the binding provisions in reflecting human rights instruments are hugely demanding for all actors in the school system. Since we are just leaving the phase of standard-setting and seriously entering the phase of implementation (Verhellen, 1997), it is understandable that almost no systematic comprehensive programmes have been set up. But some governments, some schools, some teachers, some parents and some children are addressing children's rights. Although such initiatives are somewhat piecemeal, they are characterised by high levels of commitment.

References

Blair, M. (2000) 'Race', school exclusions and human rights, in: A. Osler (ed.) *Citizenship and Democracy in Schools: diversity, identity*, equality. Stoke on Trent: Trentham.

Brock-Utne, B. (1994) Education about peace, in: D. Ray (ed.) *Education for Human Rights: an international perspective*. Paris: UNESCO.

Helio, P-L., Lawronen, E., and Bardy, M. (eds.) (1993) *Politics of Childhood and Children at Risk: provision, protection, participation*. Eurosocial Report Series, no. 45. Vienna.

Lynch, J. (1992) *Education for Citizenship in a Multicultural Society.* London: Cassell.

Richardson, R. (1991) A visitor yet a part or everybody: the tasks and goals of human rights education in: H. Starkey (ed.) *The Challenge of Human Rights Education.* London: Cassell.

Tarrow, N. (1992) Human rights education: alternative conceptions, in J. Lynch (ed.) *Cultural Diversity and the Schools, Vol. 4, Human Rights, Education and Global Responsibilities.* London: Falmer.

UNHCR (1995) *Plan of Action for the UN Decade for Human Rights Education.* Geneva: UN High Commissioner for Human Rights.

Verhellen, E. (1993) Children's rights and education: a three track legally binding imperative, *School Psychology International* 14, 199-208.

Verhellen, E. (1995) Legal Protection of children's rights, in: *Final Report of the Luxembourg Conference on the Rights of the Child in Europe: make them known, make them happen.* Luxembourg: European Forum for Child Welfare.

Verhellen, E. (ed.) (1996) *Monitoring Children's Rights.* The Hague: Kluwer Law International.

Verhellen, E. (1997) *Convention on the Rights of the Child: background, motivation, strategies, main themes.* Leuven: Garant.

Part 2

Race, Identity and Human Rights

4

Citizenship Education for a Plural Society

Peter Figueroa

The programmes of study for citizenship education (key stages 3 and 4) (DFEE/QCA, 1999) prescribe *knowledge* and *understanding* about: rights and responsibilities of citizens, consumers, employers and employees; the justice system; diversity and mutual respect; government and public services; elections and active democracy; community and voluntary work; social change; resolving conflict fairly; the media; the economy; the global community. These guidelines also prescribe *skills* of enquiry, communication, participation and responsible action, including researching and discussing topical issues, taking part in school and community based activities, and reflecting on the process of participation. However, the guidelines provide no articulated rationale, and there are some notable omissions and debatable emphases. Antiracism is hardly mentioned, and there is no sharp focus on the meaning of citizenship, on values or on developing commitment.

Any attempt to define, articulate and realise citizenship education for a plural society is challenged by the inherent complexities and the contingency of social and educational practice. I argue, however, that citizenship education for a plural society must integrate issues in citizenship, human rights and multicultural antiracism, and that any attempt to define and realise it requires philosophical analysis (focusing on key concepts and values); sociological analysis of social being and of the particular society; historical understanding; and knowledge of the particular school's ethos and practice (see Figure 4.1). This chapter thus seeks to develop a rationale for citizenship education in a plural society by exploring key concepts: citizenship, especially in a plural society; cultural pluralism; and human rights.

Citizenship

Wexler (1990: 164) argues that '...citizenship is an archaic term', according 'a sovereign individual the right... to choose on abstract and universal rather than particularist grounds... Citizenship is built on rationality and solidarity'. But with the failure of modernity, '...rationality and solidarity... seem to have disappeared' with the 'death of the individual' (Wexler, 1990: 165).

My argument is that citizenship is not an archaic term, for rationality and solidarity have not disappeared but, rather their relational character has been more fully grasped: the notion of the sovereign or absolute individual has always been fallacious. What is needed is an understanding of the citizen as an embodied individual-with-others, as an other/self. The basic human predicament is open, requiring constant conjoint application of discursive intelligence. In fact Wexler (1990: 173) seems to be calling for something very similar to this: '...a collective practice for new citizenship', which gives primacy neither to self-interest nor to speechless stupor, neither to the self nor to the other.

Van Gunsteren (1994) has attempted a synthesis of the three dominant conceptions of citizenship: the republican, the liberal and the communitarian. In the republican model, each citizen both governs and is governed. The republican virtues are: 'Courage, devotion, military discipline and statecraft' (Van Gunsteren, 1994:42). In the liberal-individualistic model the citizen is a calculating individual bearer of rights and preferences. In the communitarian model, belonging to and being moulded in terms of a historically developed community are emphasised. In Van Gunsteren's synthesis, the neo-republican conception of citizenship, the citizen is a 'member of a public community, the republic' (Van Gunsteren, 1994:45) and is socially formed. But the neo-republican virtues concern 'debating, reasonableness, democracy, choice, plurality and carefully limited use of violence' (Van Gunsteren, 1994:45). This view, although an advance, continues to assume one public community. Yet the differences between groups, communities or cultures in a plural society cannot be relegated to the 'private domain' but must be lived through in the 'public domain'.

The same problem affects all three 'models' of the national state suggested by Smith (1995: 106-107): the ethnic, civic and 'plural' models. In all three, ethnic nationalism, promulgating an ethnic canon, is seen as important for the maintenance of cohesion (see Smith, 1995: 97-102). At one extreme is 'the earlier ideal of ethnonational homogeneity and purity' (Smith, 1995: 106). Next is the civic model, with all citizens having the same universal rights by virtue of being 'bound by common laws and a shared public culture and civil religion', with other cultures likely to be subordinated or disparaged (Smith, 1995: 111). At the other extreme is the 'plural' nation. But even here the assumption seems to be that viability requires either 'a firm ethnic base' or a dominant ethnic 'public culture' (Smith, 1995:107).

For Marshall (1964) citizenship has been achieved through struggles and encompasses civil, political and social rights and duties: the rights to liberty of the person, justice, political participation, economic welfare and security, and to sharing in the social heritage. Citizenship is 'a status bestowed on those who are full members of a community', so that they are equal with respect to their rights and duties vis-à-vis each other, and have material and meaningful relations with others in the community to which they belong (1964: 84). Citizenship requires a bond involving 'a direct sense of community membership based on loyalty to a civilisation which is a common possession' (ibid.: 92).

According to Oldfield (1990), the political community, that is the community of which one may be a citizen, has three constitutive characteristics: autonomy of the individual citizens, friendship or 'concord', and judgement or practical wisdom. Autonomy means potential for self-determination or the power for self-choosing. Concord means a sense of responsibility towards fellow citizens, a sense of mutual interdependence. Judgement refers to the judgements that people make about the rules that are to be authoritative in their community, and especially to the judgements 'which provide the community... with its identity' (Oldfield, 1990: 27), the 'we' judgements. Oldfield says that 'political identity... must result from self-conscious deliberation and judgement, and must also be expressive of an ethical commitment.... It is this which constitutes citizenship' (ibid.: 26). Moreover, only 'a religion limited to the nation', which elevates the fatherland into '...the object of the citizens' adoration' (ibid.: 73) could generate the necessary patriotism.

Marshall's, Smith's and Oldfield's views, however, present many difficulties, especially with reference to the plural society. Whose judgements are to count as 'we' judgements? What exactly is intended by the 'direct sense of community membership based on loyalty to a civilisation which is a common possession' (Marshall, 1964: 92)? Is there an assumption of one (public), fixed, homogeneous social and cultural heritage? Are this culture and the 'civil religion' above open to question or to reinterpretation and change? Rather than being monolithic, must not this shared social heritage encompass the actual diversity of the society? Do minorities, or those with little or no power, have the same basic rights as others? For what do their judgements count? Is autonomy absolute, the power of sovereign individuals? Do not citizens have rights and duties vis-à-vis non-citizens, at least as fellow humans?

The notion that the 'body politic' can only hold together if the members of the society adhere to a civil religion (Rousseau, 1968) in which the fatherland itself is adored, is an absolutist, nationalist, ethnocentric view, which puts a premium on conformity and leads to cultural imperialism, fascism, racism and war. It is also self-defeating, for it sets community against community and threatens the very happiness and security that, according to Rousseau, membership in society was intended to ensure. It threatens the freedom to be different, by requiring submission to a supreme state and to a sacred public culture. Likewise, the liberal-individualist tradition, in which the individual is seen as a one-dimensional absolute, is self-defeating, for it sets individual against individual. These views have no notion of multiple worlds, multiple identities or situated freedom.

What rather needs developing is a genuine 'plural' model, not one, like Smith's (1995), requiring either 'a firm ethnic base' or a dominant ethnic 'public culture'. Social cohesion, the unity of the nation, should be built through and around the democratic sharing of a complex, different/similar, political, social and economic process/ system. In other words, a type of national identity is called for which rests not on the assumption of one (dominant) canon, ethnic or civic, but rather on the notion of multiple identities, multiple realities, process. By its nature, the 'plural model' is one which needs constantly to be re-worked.

Human Rights

First, though, the notion of human rights must receive some consideration. What exactly is the nature of a human right; what is the rationale for this notion? Human rights can be thought of as basic entitlements, that is, as what is due to any person as a human being, and what, as a human being, any person may be or do without let or hindrance. To this extent they may be thought of as minimal requirements of how we should treat, and not treat, each other, and allow each other to be and act.

Although it is inherently difficult to establish, it seems to me that such human rights are based on, or assume, some notion of the human being as such as being of unique worth, and being autonomous (though 'autonomous-with-others', not absolutely). Against Perry (1998), I reject, however, a necessarily religious basis to human rights. The important point is that every human is intrinsically an end rather than a means, that human life cannot be satisfactorily understood without the assumption of human being as intrinsically 'of worth'.

It is on this basis that human rights rest. But these rights are not absolute in the sense that the rights of each are situated in relation to and limited by the rights of everyone else. For instance, to say that you have a right to free speech entails that I have a duty to respect –

and even to promote – it. However, since I too have a right to free speech, and you a duty to respect and even promote it, and since, moreover, we each have a right to basic respect as humans and each a duty to respect the other (and ourselves), your right to free speech and my right to free speech is limited. An absolutist and sovereignly individualistic human rights discourse can be counterproductive, leading to conflict by neglecting responsibilities and mutuality. Human rights are the rights of concrete individuals-with-others.

Besides, as Perry remarks (1998:64), there is 'pluralism about human goods'. Although human beings are alike in certain ways, some treatments being bad for all of them (for example, torture) and some good for all (for example, love), there are nevertheless many differences between human beings, certain things being good for some but not for others, while some things are bad for some but not for others. Moreover, there are many alternative goods. Each might be a (possible) good for any human being, but no one person can realise them all. As Perry (1998:65) says: 'A conception of human good... can be... universalist as well as pluralist: It can acknowledge sameness as well as difference, commonality as well as variety'.

Cultural Pluralism

All present-day societies (if not, indeed, all societies) are plural, even if in varying ways and to varying degrees – plural, for instance, along dimensions of 'ethnicity', class, gender, age, education, power, individual difference and especially culture. Culture is a complicated and wide-ranging concept encompassing 'a distinct 'whole way of life' and 'artistic and intellectual activities', including 'all the 'signifying practices'', such as the arts, philosophy and journalism (Williams, 1981:13). The guiding spirit of the particular way of life is central to culture, tending to give broad direction and informing intellectual, artistic and social activity. Also central to culture is the shared system of symbols through which the participants in that culture interact. Thus culture includes: cognitive elements (for example, concepts, symbols, theoretical systems, beliefs, knowledge); linguistic systems which realise these in organised and communicative forms; value orientations, normative patterns; and social organisational rules, kinship rules and the like.

However, culture must not be reified. As Günter Lenz (1993: 48) argues, it needs to be understood as 'a polyvocal, contested, complex process of the construction and deconstruction of meanings and identities... in and through the dialogues, the interactions, and the relations of power...'. Still, even though identities and meanings are 'full of contradictions and changes' (Lenz, 1993: 48), culture is also, through sedimentation, history and the given context, largely system-like. Neither the individual nor the group is completely free to 'negotiate' meanings and identities 'at will'. Culture refers, then, both to process and to the meanings and patterns generated and sustained by the continuing process.

The term cultural pluralism, often used interchangeably with multiculturalism, can be used either descriptively or to express an ideal. In the descriptive sense, a culturally plural society is one in which more or less distinctive cultures live side by side, a multicultural society. However, these cultures interact, mutually defining each other and themselves. As Lenz says (1993: 54), 'cultural identities are continually constructed and revised in processes of intra- and intercultural interactions'. Every culture is itself an interculture (Lenz, 1993), encompassing deep diversity.

The experience of the other, the different other, is at the heart of the human experience. It is through this experience that the individual, a society or a culture comes to self-awareness and achieves an identity. It is not the self, nor the social, but the interrelationship between the other and the self which is primary (see Baccarini, 1995). The human person is an 'individual' who is inseparably a social being. People do not initially come together because of some contingent 'social contract'. They are inseparable from one another. They gain their origin, being, culture and identity in and through interaction with each other, while nevertheless retaining their difference. Interdependence and social situatedness are fundamental. As Twine (1994:11) puts it:

> Each is dependent on the other for the development of his or her 'self'. ...the 'social self' is constructed from a network of social relationships, past and present. It is neither fully autonomous nor fully determined.... freedom as 'self-development' comes from social membership and participation.

Inseparably, the experience of the other (person, society or culture) is experience of difference and also of similarity, of the other as at least human: I experience my being as human in experiencing the being of the other as human. Central in the experience of the self, of the other, of culture, is the experience of disjuncture/unity, of inter-dependence. I experience myself as complex, as multiple, as having several identities, as fulfilling many roles, as interrelating in different ways to several others. Both culture and identity are multiple.

Far from diversity being disintegrative or a fault to be overcome, the experience of the different is primary, and a rich resource. What matters is how the diversity is articulated with other factors such as the distribution of status, resources and power, and how it is perceived and evaluated. The plural society can have a national identity which includes diversity, a respect for difference and a valuing of pluralism. A society remains maximally viable only if its diversity, if its difference/similarity, is respected and dealt with in various constructive ways.

This is cultural pluralism as an ideal: appreciating the strengths of difference and diversity, and promoting constructive interrelations between cultures, groups and individuals. This is a positive, though critical, approach to difference/similarity, to the basic reality of dynamic interrelationship. Here the term interculturalism is sometimes used. Cultural pluralism as an ideal assumes as basic certain social and political values such as: the right and freedom to be different; openness; equity; justice; solidarity; rationality; the democratic right of all to contribute equitably to shaping society; and conversely the need to combat both imposed assimilation and divisiveness – racism, injustice, inequality and discrimination.

Pluralism does not assume that all people are contingently the same, however, or that *de facto* they enjoy equal power, status or resources. Rather, pluralism sets equity – not simply sameness – as a social ideal. It assumes that people *qua* people are equal, that as human beings they are fundamentally comparable to each other and are basically of equal worth.

It likewise assumes that each culture, developed to deal with the human predicament in specific situations, has at least a basic worth and is deserving of respect. It is assumed that each culture, including my own, has strong points and weak points, and that if I were to look from the point of view of the other, I might be able to see the strength of their 'case' and the weaknesses of my own – and conversely, they might be able to see the weaknesses of theirs and the strengths of mine.

Pluralism does not mean a radical relativism. That would be self-defeating. One must stand somewhere. It is not possible to stand nowhere. But neither is an attempt to stand everywhere tenable. I can realise that all cultures have claims – *and* that all cultures are bounded and open to error. But I cannot commit myself to all cultures at the same time. However, committing myself to one culture – and I cannot avoid doing so – is to commit myself to culture; committing myself to my truth is to commit myself to truth. Truths can only be focused on through particular lenses; it is nevertheless truth that is focused on, however distorting the lenses might be.

Put another way, the binary opposition of particularism/universalism must be questioned. One must reject a universalism which is nothing more than a generalisation of one's own specificity: the self as absolute. But equally one must reject a particularism which insists that no one can be like me: the difference as absolute. Any universal truth is only expressed in some particular truth.

Rather than relativism, pluralism implies relationalism. This means a basic recognition of difference/similarity, of the individual as a divided unity and of the community as a togetherness of different individuals, groups and interests. It implies a commitment to meaning and openness in meaning; a commitment to truth *and* perspectivism. A provisional affirmation subject to further comparison, a questioning of views, a shifting of focus, a self-correcting and mutually correcting process of enquiry – are all involved; and always implicit is the notion of what is true or right, and a search for it. People do choose. The point is that choice is concrete and that at the point of choice I am convinced that one alternative is better than another. I can only act – and think – by committing myself to certain values and truths; but I realise that, whatever my present commitment, I might be mistaken. However, this is not a matter of whim; if I come to realise that I was mistaken, it will be for a reason. In other words, a rational and critical discourse is fundamental, but one that is situated, on-going, self-evaluating.

Of course, there can be conflicts of values, of cultures, of rights; and there are genuine dilemmas facing cultural pluralism. For instance, since it propounds openness to all cultures, how can it deal with a culture which rejects openness? However, the principle is that openness and situated, bounded rationality do not mean accepting any position proffered but mean instead being willing to give a genuine hearing to the reasons for any position held. The respect that cultural pluralism calls for is critical respect. The critique must be carried out in practice. The outcome cannot be guaranteed. But there is an 'ultimate court': that is reason, everyone's and any one's reason, in practice. Ultimately, differences and problems must be resolved by discourse – if they are not to be dealt with by violence. The process must be constant and constantly renewed.

Citizenship In A Plural Society

What then does citizenship, in particular citizenship in a plural society, imply? It implies, I argue, most of the specific features mentioned by Marshall, Oldfield and Van Gunsteren's synthesis, but understood in pluralist, relational, not absolutist, terms. Thus it means rights and responsibilities, but bounded in social, contingent situations. Similarly, autonomy is the ability to decide and act 'independently', but not in a vacuum, absolutely or arbitrarily. Also, each group has the right to its identity, to self-determination, but in interdependence and conjunction with other groups, with each member contributing.

Mutuality or 'concord' implies, both at the individual and the group levels, constructive interaction, solidarity, deciding and acting in such a way as to take account of each other appropriately. It implies an assertion of the self, a forging of the self and the other in relation to each other, and a commitment to the community as a whole, but not a blind commitment to one's people or to some supposed monolithic heritage.

Judgement or practical wisdom too is culturally, historically and socially situated. It is lived rationality in action, always situated and exercised in specific contexts and always open to error and to revision. It is self-corrective, and implicitly takes different points of view into account. Although fallible, it is as judgement, committed to truthfulness and rightness.

Thus, citizenship (in a plural society) involves: commitment to the society in its diversity; openness to, and indeed solidarity with and respect for, the different other, in particular the 'ethnically' different; acceptance of the basic equal worth of all people, of the rights and responsibilities of all; and a rejection of any form of exploitation, inequitable treatment or racism. It means a taking account of difference where that is appropriate, but not where it is not.

But none of this implies a blind commitment to 'the common good'. Citizenship in a plural society implies a security in one's own culture – but not an unquestioning security. It also implies a *critical* respect for the culture, beliefs and values of the other even in their difference, a critical respect for difference. Rational dialogue (that is, meaningful exchange of views, not monologue, nor command, nor wilful, blind or spiteful discourse) between the different parties is essential, so that all may equitably contribute to the decisions taken and the judgements made. The sort of patriotism implied by the position I have outlined is a lived, dynamic commitment, a commitment which is amenable to fallible reflection and reason, a commitment which can be focused, differentiated, re-directed, even corrected.

Citizenship In Plural Britain

Britain is plural not only because it contains several more or less coherent ethnic minority communities or cultures with their origins in the Indian sub-continent, Africa and the Caribbean in particular – the 'visible' ethnic minorities. There is also a great deal of diversity within these visible ethnic minorities – as also within the majority sector (based, for example, on region, social class and gender). But there are also significant 'invisible' ethnic minorities, white ethnic minority groups, originating, for example, in Ireland, North America, continental Europe, South Africa, Australia and New Zea-

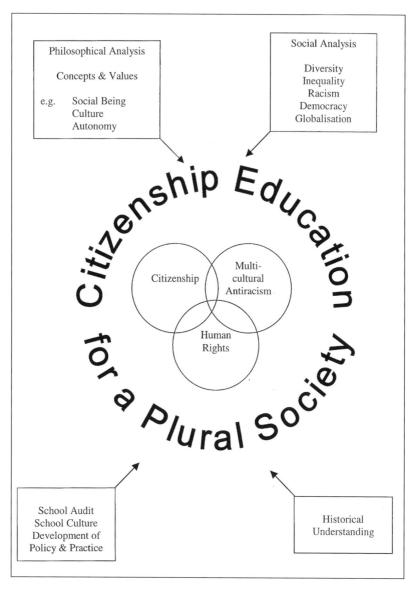

Figure 4.1: Defining and articulating citizenship education of a plural society

land. Furthermore, the visible ethnic minorities experience inequity and racism in different forms (see for example, Figueroa, 1991 and Modood *et al*, 1997). Racism at the cultural and structural levels, the racist frame-of-reference, code or ideology, and the unequal distribution of power, resources or goods along lines socially constructed as 'racial', are inescapable. Equally, the society has strong democratic traditions. An understanding of British and European history of the last five centuries – for example, the growth of nationalism and capitalism, slavery, colonisation, Empire, the British Raj in India, decolonisation, civil rights movements, and post-war labour migration – is important for comprehending British and other European societies today, their diversity, inequalities, racism, and democratic structures, and the deep legitimacy of the citizenship rights of 'minorities'. Finally, citizenship must also be seen in the context of globalisation.

For everyone, including the minorities, to enjoy full citizenship, the inequities, racism and discrimination must be combated. Recognising that there are different forms of racism can help policy makers and schools identify and deal with these phenomena. Positive strategies must include the promotion of such values as equity, anti-racism and openness. It is also important to be constantly seeking equitable, peaceful and positive ways of avoiding, anticipating or resolving the miscommunications, conflicts, racism or other problems which arise.

We must learn to benefit from the diversity of riches, to identify the commonalities, agreements and differences – and to agree to differ about the disagreements. The worth of each community must be accepted, and every individual, community and culture must be able to contribute to the agreed values and social and political arrangements. Diversity must be publicly recognised and respected, 'given public status and dignity' (Parekh, 1991:197). Plural Britain needs to 'develop a new social and cultural policy capable of nurturing ethnic identities...' (Parekh, 1991:197). As Modood *et al* (1997) put it: 'an explicit idea of multi-cultural citizenship needs to be formulated for Britain'. 'British' must be seen as fully including the ethnic minority cultures and communities. But the minority communities being seen as British does not imply their denying their 'ethnic' origins and identity: multiple identity, for individuals and communities, must be recognised and accepted.

Citizenship Education For A Plural Society

The implications of these various observations are far-reaching and complex, and can barely be indicated here. Other chapters in this volume present greater details. Education is only one set of the range of social policies and programmes that are needed. Moreover, teaching and learning take place in all spheres of daily life, so that the educational implications extend far beyond schools. And since educational institutions are an integral part of society, inequalities in schools may be a symptom and consequence of wider inequalities, and will in turn contribute to those inequalities. Educational inequalities therefore need specifically to be addressed. As good as a school's citizenship education arrangements may be, the future of the students as citizens, and of civic society, will be compromised if the students do not receive an education which permits them to develop their potential and to play a fulfilling and gainful part in society. The implications for schools are not limited to pedagogical and curricular matters but impinge on all other aspects – ethos, organisation, administration, inspection, personnel, relationships between and among teachers and students, the roles students can play, physical environment, assessment, selection, the pastoral system and extra-curricular activities.

As indicated, citizenship in a plural society implies a whole array of aspects, such as: the experience of difference and reciprocity; situated rights and duties; certain lived, relational and democratic virtues; a pluralistic outlook; a rejection of racism and any form of exploitation. It is the task of citizenship education for plural Britain to contribute to the formation of citizens in all the various aspects. The contents and methods used must be compatible with and geared towards the aims and ideals of citizenship for a plural society. Each student must learn to take responsibility for the tasks they need to perform as students and in their everyday lives, and for developing the necessary competences. The development of knowledge, understanding and skills is necessary; but so too is the development of the relevant values, attitudes, competences, behavioural patterns and commitment. A central part of citizenship education is exploring and discussing the key concepts, values and issues, and coming to grips with their practical everyday implications. Topical issues, such as asylum seekers, racism and local or general elections, need to be addressed in an informed and mature way. The discussion can go in-depth on the basis of a limited number of specific, well-chosen examples. Some topical issues from other countries, or different approaches to similar issues in different countries, might be addressed. Schools can teach citizenship education for a plural society and promote a commitment to human rights, antiracism and the democratic values directly through focused sessions in citizen-ship education, Personal, Social and Health Education (PSHE), moral education and other subjects and through assemblies and projects; and indirectly through the hidden curriculum, the ethos, equitable relations between the members of the school community, and democratic practices and structures, such as a school council.

The task is not easy. The challenges are large and varied and are coterminous with social being itself. Existing power relations and sedimented culture mean that individuals and groups operate within the taken-for-granted perspectives and imperatives of existing cul-tural 'habits' and frames (Figueroa, 1991). These need to be brought to awareness and subverted, but in constructive and reconstructive ways.

References

Baccarini, E. (1995) The identity between specificities and universality: the problem of minorities, in: D. Dadsi (general rapporteur) *Specificities and Univer-sality: problems of identities*. Strasbourg: Council of Europe.

Department for Education and Employment/Qualifications and Curriculum Authority (1999) *The National Curriculum: handbook for secondary teachers in England, Key Stages 3 and 4*. Norwich: HMSO.

Figueroa, P. (1991) *Education and the Social Construction of 'Race'*. London: Routledge.

Figueroa, P (1999) Multiculturalism and antiracism in a new ERA: a critical review. *Race Ethnicity and Education*, 2 (2): 281-301.

Hymes, D. (1972) Introduction, in C. Cazden, V. John and D. Hymes (eds.) *Fuctions of Language in the classroom*. New York: Teachers College Press.

Lenz, G. H. (1993) Multicultural critique and the new American Studies, in: H. Bak (ed.) *Multiculturalism and the Canon of American Culture*. Amsterdam: Vu University Press.

Marshall, T. H. (1964) *Class, Citizenship, and Social Development*. Garden City, N.Y.: Doubleday and Co.

Modood, T., Berthoud, R., Lakey, J., Nazroo, J., Smith, P., Virdee, S. and Beishon, S. (1997) *Ethnic Minorities in Britain: Diversity and Disadvantage (The Fourth National Survey of Ethnic Minorities)*. London: Policy Studies Institute.

Oldfield, A. (1990) *Citizenship and Community: civic republicanism and the modern world*. London: Routledge.

Parekh, B. (1991) British citizenship and cultural difference, in: G. Andrews (ed.) *Citizenship*. London: Lawrence and Wishart.

Perry, M. J. (1998) *The Idea of Human Rights: four inquiries*. New York: Oxford University Press.

Rousseau, J-J. (1968) *The Social Contract* (ed. M. Cranston). Harmondsworth: Penguin.

Smith, A. D. (1995) *Nations and Nationalism in a Global Era*. Cambridge: Polity Press.

Twine, F. (1994) *Citizenship and Social Rights: the interdependence of self and society*. London: Sage.

Van Gunsteren, H. (1994) Four conceptions of citizenship, in: B. van Steenbergen (ed.) *The Condition of Citizenship*. London: Sage.

Wexler, P. (1990) Citizenship in the semiotic society, in: B. S. Turner (ed.) *Theories of Modernity and Postmodernity*. London: Sage.

Williams, R. (1981) *Culture*. Glasgow: Fontana.

5

Human Rights, Cultures and Language Teaching

Michael Byram and Manuela Guilherme

We argue in this chapter that there is a reciprocal relation-ship between human rights education (including citizen-ship education) and foreign language-and-culture educa-tion. On the one hand, the concept of human rights can offer an anti-relativist standpoint important for the study of and encounter with other cultural values, meanings and behaviours. On the other hand, foreign language-and-culture education can provide the means of decentring, and the critical cultural awareness which allows learners to reflect critically on their own society and their own values, mean-ings and behaviours within it.

Education for Citizenship in International Perspective
In his discussion of cultural pluralism, by which he implies pluralism within one society rather than across a number of societies, Figueroa, in the previous chapter of this volume, places emphasis on the power of rational critical discourse to establish respect for diversity. He also stresses the existence of meta-universals experienced through com-mitment to a culture which is simultaneously the experience of culture. He takes this stance by insisting that all cultures have within them the possibility of rational self- and other evaluation on the basis of available facts and arguments. A similar position is argued by Mendus (1995) with particular relevance to British society.

Figueroa goes on to make a distinction between relativism and relationalism, and to consider the response people may have to experiences of other cultures or values, meanings and behaviours. His argument is that people make choices, but on the basis of understanding the strength and weakness of the values of others' and also of one's own culture. Here there is a potential link with foreign language-and-culture teaching, since the others in question need not simply be in one's own society, on which Figueroa concentrates, but also in other societies, which themselves will be pluri-cultural/lingual and hopefully pluralist.

In his discussion of citizenship, Figueroa develops a 'plural model':

> Social cohesion, the unity of the nation, should be built through and around the democratic sharing of a complex, different/similar, political, social and economic process/system. In other words, a type of national identity is called for which rests not on the assumption of one (dominant) canon, ethnic or civic, but rather on the notion of multiple identities, multiple realities, process. By its nature, the 'plural model' is one which needs constantly to be re-worked. (2000: 51)

Again, a foreign language-and-culture perspective can and should be introduced here. The question which needs to be asked is whether one of the multiple identities should go beyond the national level, to include an international identity. Clearly, within the European context, there is a wide expectation that there should also be a 'European identity' and a sense of 'European citizenship'. This expectation is to be found in both European Union and Council of Europe documents, although with different emphases and interpretations.

The Council of Europe has recently begun vigorously to pursue the issues of 'education for democratic citizenship', as a result of the Final Declaration of the Second Summit of Heads of State and Governments in November 1997. This includes a project with the title 'Education for Democratic Citizenship', in which Audigier offers a definition of the 'competences' of the democratic citizen (here presented in abbreviated form):

cognitive competences:

- legal and political: knowledge of rules of collective life

- understanding of power in a democratic society

- knowledge of the present world: historical and cultural dimension

- capacity for critical analysis

- knowledge of the principles and values of human rights and democratic citizenship: based on concept of freedom and equal dignity

affective competences and choice of values:

- the importance of conviction and adherence to principles

- thinking of oneself as an individual in relation to others

- belonging to a group or groups

- a personal and collective affective dimension

- values of freedom, equality and solidarity

- positive acceptance of differences and diversity

- beyond a narrow conception of tolerance

capacities for action (social competences):

- capacity to live with others and cooperate: construct and implement joint projects

- capacity to resolve conflicts in accordance with the principles of democratic law: calling on a third person

- capacity to take part in public debate: argue and choose in a real life situation (Audigier, 1998).

It might be argued, however, that there is insufficient regard here for the international and interlingual nature of being a citizen in Europe or in any similar context where public debate or 'the capacity to live with others' involves interaction through another language. Furthermore, we would argue, it cannot be taken for granted that the presuppositions of debate and interaction are identical in other cultures. Thus the democratic citizen in such contexts needs communicative competence in another language and also intercultural competence.

This is also often the case within one society but is seldom taken into account; it seems to be simply assumed that the dominant language of the society will be adequate for a plural model of national citizenship (Rassool, 1998). One of the advantages of foreign language-and-culture education is to make the weakness of this taken-for-granted view self-evident.

We have to turn to a global vision of the nature and purposes of education, the UNESCO report (Delors, 1996) for an attempt to ensure that citizenship and 'learning to live together', as one of the 'four pillars of learning', involves not just those people in one's own society, whether national or international, but everyone. Nonetheless, implications for language learning are still not made clear.

Finally, we wish to argue that the extension of a plural model of citizenship and identity to an international level – whether European or global – involves necessarily the consideration of foreign language-and-culture learning. First, it offers a perspective which supports and makes more evident the implications of what Figueroa calls a relationalist position. Second, it provides the competence, intercultural and communicative, which is a pragmatic necessity.

Human Rights, Citizenship and Foreign Language/ Culture Education

The notions of human rights and citizenship have developed in modern societies in connection with the ideal of equality. Human rights has consisted of a moral/universal discourse that, on the one hand, has often included the dissemination, sometimes the imposition of a western, often eurocentric vision of society and, on the other hand, of the request for the concession of rights which hardly surpass those indispensable for basic survival. Therefore, human rights has been, on the whole, a rather abstract moral discourse to be largely exported – in other words, from 'us' to 'them'. In addition, citizenship has also been 'an emblem of modernity' in that it translates into practice the concept of equality of individuals united by civil contract before the state (Wexler, 1993: 164). Since it has been closely linked with the organisation of the nation-state, it has meant, on the one hand, the enjoyment of civil, political and social rights and, on the other hand, it has been geared to the ideal of cultural homogeneity. This has resulted in a model of democracy that relies on a common public sphere based on homogeneous cultural representations and general interests, while cultural differences are kept to a private sphere (Young, 1998; Hall 2000).

Contemporary political philosophy, however, has put into question the modern conceptualisation both of the self and of the interaction between different 'selves', as well as the modern formulation of the concept of equality, and this may have a strong impact in the perception of human rights and of citizenship. At the same time, the mental, social, political and economic institutions we live with, which are legacies of the Enlightenment tradition, are being challenged both by the formation of overarching political and economic structures emerging from globalising influences and by international mobility and consequent acculturation and cross-culturalisation of citizens, together with the strengthening of ethnic communities. Consequently, whereas the most cherished legacy of the Enlightenment tradition was the quest for equality, the main concern today is how to deal with difference by making sure there is equity and equivalence.

For example, Habermas' moral universalism relies on an 'intersubjectively recognised self-identification' accomplished 'on the basis of the intersubjective recognition of reciprocal self-representations' (Habermas, 1979: 107). This perspective reinforces a subject-subject type of interaction where 'moral questions, like ethical questions, must be addressed from the perspective of the participants', that is, they are negotiated within symmetrical communication (Habermas, 1993: 24). Furthermore, the development of the concept of equality throughout modernity and its consequences in the organisation of society has been much challenged by postmodernism and multiculturalism since both emphasise differentiation. According to Lyotard, modernity made the specific and the particular depend on broader and more abstract objectives, that is, on totalising myths that silenced the counter- and micro-narratives. Lyotard identifies the postmodern condition as the process of 'delegitimation' of such metadiscourses (Lyotard, 1986). Moreover, postmodern deconstructionism is a useful political tool for multicultural democracies because it entails a 'deep restructuring of relations of recognition' (Fraser, 1998: 35). This means that it relies not only on differentiation between groups but also on hyperdifferentiation, that is, on differentiation within and across groups.

A cultural politics of difference has, therefore, problematised issues of institutional access and representation in that the fragmentation of the self and of social and cultural life together with a different articulation between the global and the local require a different approach to these issues. Not only may the citizen apply for membership of and protection from a myriad of local, national and transnational organisations (Giddens, 2000), but also s/he may have her/his multiple private/public identities represented in the political arena at different levels. The demands for active citizenship, from this perspective, do not stop within the limits of instrumental citizenship, in terms of the enjoyment of political rights of representation, but aim for a more intense exercise of citizenship. In addition, the idea of a decentered self that runs through all post-structuralist and postmodern theories animates the subject to enjoy disparate experiences without the preoccupation of achieving a self-contained, unitary and final condition. From this perspective, all circles of identity formation are likely to create legitimate identifications that weave together.

Within this context, foreign language-and-culture education may contribute significantly to both human rights education and citizenship education, since it provides space for reflecting on the ways knowledge and culture are constructed according to contingent and transitory historical constraints. By juxtaposing two or more realities where cultural/political articulations were accomplished differently, it is possible to raise awareness of the limits of traditions on both sides and provide some grounds for critical cultural revitalisation, transgression and creativity. It is the task of foreign language-and-culture education to interrogate dominant and subordinate ideologies, to give 'voice' to the discourses that have been silenced and to the particular narratives of the students, and to make connections between different narratives at both local and global levels. This is not only an epistemological but also a social, political and ethical enterprise, since it engages with education for self and social change. Critical intercultural learning involves more than experiencing, interpreting and accommodating to other cultures; it entails making connections, exploring articulations and changing representations. Therefore, it has profound implications for the way students construct their cultural identities and, consequently, for the way they respond to their everyday lives.

As a cultural worker (Giroux, 1992), the foreign language-and-culture teacher may transform the hermeneutic exploration of a foreign code into an act of cultural creation by investing her/his students with the power to share intercultural events critically, interrogate their own and others' histories and commit themselves to the responsibility of building this intercultural world. By critically understanding the organisation of meanings and interests in particular cultural codes and how those reflect particular configurations of knowledge and power, students, while studying a foreign culture, will critically recognise some of the preoccupations, desires, successes and challenges they face in their everyday lives. This process enables students to make informed choices about their lives and, above all, it makes them aware that they are entitled to a choice. By becoming critically aware of the multiple levels of their cultural and political identities, teachers and students may develop a desire to be involved in political decisions and in ethical issues as well as commitment to engage in transformative action (Guilherme, 2000).

Likewise, the teaching/learning about foreign languages/cultures is enriched if it considers human rights education and education for democratic citizenship as broader educational frameworks to which they should permanently refer. These should form an influential and consistent contribution to foreign language-and-culture education and should be included as major components in the corresponding teachers' development (Osler and Starkey, 1996). Teachers of foreign language-and-culture themselves need to be educated about human rights and democratic citizenship because they deal with issues of identity, difference, equality, equivalence and equity, and are responsible for the preparation of democratic global citizens/

intercultural speakers. Yet as our research shows, there is only minimal awareness of this (Byram and Risager, 1999).

More specifically, human rights may provide foreign language-and-culture education with culture-universals, basic principles, and values that traverse cultures. However, these should not remain as abstract notions and the study of documents produced by international organisations is fundamental (Osler and Starkey, 1996). Education for citizenship, by acknowledging local, national and global levels, also deals with the relationship between culture-universals and culture-specifics (Brislin and Yoshida, 1994). In consequence, foreign language-and-culture education becomes involved in the discussion about the complexities of the interaction between culture-universals and culture-specifics that make issues of human rights and citizenship more difficult today. By being placed within these general frameworks, foreign language-and-culture education will foster the development of critical cultural awareness of both target and native cultures. In this instance, equal rights are confronted with the right to difference, the search for consensus with the inevitability of dissensus, the striving after progress as a linear continuum with the potentialities of relativism that works within networks of power, and the vigour of individual emancipation with the motivating force of solidarity. The negotiation between antithetical modes such as equality/difference, consensus/dissent, progress/relativism, emancipation/solidarity improves the comprehension of cultural complexities and allows for some flexibility in understanding intra- and inter-cultural interactions. Furthermore, education for democratic citizenship, within a broader framework of human rights, clarifies and reinforces the political nature and purpose of foreign language/culture education (Byram and Risager, 1999). It is to a more detailed discussion of the relationship at a pedagogical level that we turn next.

Critical Cultural Awareness in Foreign Language-and-Culture Education
The intercultural speaker

Foreign language teaching (FLT) has been dominated for the past two decades and more by the phrase 'communicative competence' taken from Hymes' work: his emphasis on appropriateness, on the ability to know *when* and *how* to use language and not just the ability to use it accurately according to norms set by native speakers. What is perhaps remarkable is the way in which Hymes' view that 'judgement of appropriateness may not be assigned to different spheres, as between the linguistic and the cultural' (Hymes, 1972: 286) has been largely ignored. There has been more emphasis on sociolinguistic than sociocultural appropriateness, perhaps because of the influence of speech act theory and discourse analysis. As a consequence FLT has remained concerned with the inculcation of 'skills' and, in its focus on technical issues, forgotten that communication is not just a matter of passing information or obtaining goods and services, but of interacting with other human beings in socially complex and rich environments.

If this technicist approach is replaced by a richer and more complex view of interaction through a foreign language, then the relationship with human rights education soon becomes clear. (Incidentally, it also takes us back to some of the pre-communicative purposes of foreign language education, to introduce learners to other civilisations and cultures, but usually high Cultures.) Through foreign language education, learners have the opportunity to engage with people with other values, meanings and behaviours, potentially but not necessarily in a pluralist mode as described here by Figueroa, for a multicultural society.

Another of the problems created by the adoption of Hymes' account of communicative competence in FLT is that he was describing the acquisition of first languages and, moreover, by monolingual speakers. So foreign language theory continued to be dominated by a model of native or first language speakers, who are monolingual, an ideal to which learners were expected to aspire and against which they were measured. Yet it is neither possible for foreign language learners to acquire the technical competence of the native speaker – assuming that the definition of the native speaker is not problematic, which is not a justified assumption, in fact – nor is it desirable that learners attempt to adopt an identity which is an imitation of a monolingual native speaker.

What is required rather is a model of an 'intercultural speaker' (Byram and Zarate, 1997; Byram, 1997), someone with 'intercultural communicative competence'. An intercultural speaker has some of the skills and knowledge of the native speaker – for example linguistic/grammatical competence – and others which are specific to being a speaker of a foreign language and involved in interactions across cultural and linguistic boundaries. In brief, intercultural communicative competence can be defined in terms of a number of competences, some of them linguistic ('linguistic', 'sociolinguistic', 'discourse') others cultural (represented in Figure 5.1 within the circle) defined as:

- *Attitudes (savoir être)*: curiosity and openness, readiness to suspend disbelief about other cultures and belief about one's own

- *Knowledge (savoirs)*: of social groups and their products and practices in one's own and in one's interlocutor's country, and of the general processes of societal and individual interaction

- *Skills of interpreting and relating (savoir comprendre)*: ability to interpret a document or event from another culture, to explain it and relate it to documents or events from one's own

- *Skills of discovery and interaction (savoir apprendre et faire)*: ability to acquire new knowledge of a culture and cultural practices and the ability to operate knowledge, attitudes and skills under the constraints of real-time communication and interaction

- *Critical cultural awareness/political education (savoir s'engager)*: an ability to evaluate, critically and on the basis of explicit criteria, perspectives, practices and products in one's own and other cultures and countries.

It is the final '*savoir*' which is our concern on this occasion. On the one hand, it is the aim of language teaching that intercultural speakers should be people who can decentre and see the relativity of

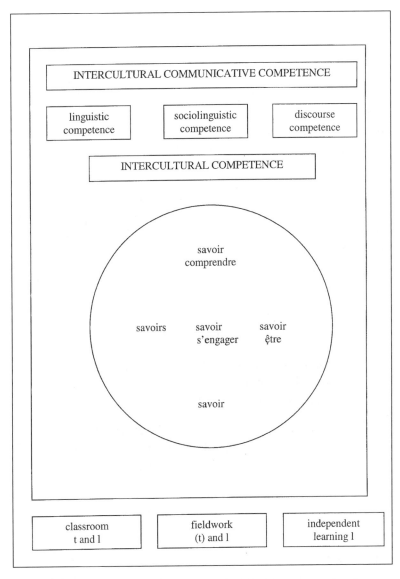

Figure 5.1: Competencies in foreign language-and-culture education

their own (and others') apparently 'natural' and taken for granted meanings, values and behaviours. On the other hand, if learners are not to descend into relativism as a consequence, they need to have a clear standpoint, which is nonetheless governed by what Figueroa calls the 'ultimate court': that is reason, everyone's and any one's reason, in practice' (this volume: 56). Reason determines that: 'One must stand somewhere. It is not possible to stand nowhere. But neither is an attempt to stand everywhere tenable' (Figueroa, 2000: 55).

So what we are arguing is that foreign language education has a moral and political potential, one which is not widely accepted in Britain but which is present in other countries, notably in Portugal (Guilherme, 2000).

Furthermore, Doyé (1993) has argued that there are links between teaching for intercultural competence and political education. He quotes Gagel, who argues that political education underpins all education. Political education has three broad aims:

- cognitive orientation, meaning the acquisition of concepts, knowledge and modes of thinking relevant to the comprehension of political phenomena

- evaluative orientation, meaning the clarification and mediation of values, and the development of a capacity for political judgements on the basis of these values

- an action orientation, meaning education into the capacity and willingness for political engagement.

Doyé argues that there is congruence with the aims of foreign language teaching. The first, the cognitive, corresponds to the giving of information about and understanding of other cultures. The second, the evaluative, corresponds to the desire to make learners aware of and have respect for the values of other people and cultures. With respect to action orientation, both political education and foreign language teaching attempt to involve learners in engagement with others, in the first case in one's own society, in the second in another society.

A similar link between language teaching and human rights education is suggested by Starkey who says:

> In recent years the priority for linguists has been how to teach languages effectively, rather than with the content of this teaching. On the other hand, some of those concerned with promoting in schools the common European values of social justice, democracy and respect for human rights and the rule of law have largely neglected the teaching of languages as a vehicle for these concerns. (Starkey, 1996: 114)

What we are suggesting then is that we should be developing not just cultural awareness but *critical* cultural awareness. Doyé points out that in the English tradition the phrase 'political education' is avoided, perhaps for fear of an association with 'indoctrination'. This is, however, discussed in the Crick Report (QCA, 1998), even though this document lacks proper consideration of the nature of international citizenship and of the significance of language learning and intercultural competence. Consequently, the new interpretation in England of education for citizenship, which corresponds to the German concept of *politische Bildung*, equally lacks full consideration of an international dimension to citizenship.

It is crucial to 'critical cultural awareness' that there be a standpoint – and human rights offers one. No doubt, in other societies other standpoints may be taken and, no doubt, some teachers will want to propose their own standpoint. However, the latter point is highly contentious and in our view the teacher should not be imposing their own standpoint but making learners be explicit about theirs, about its implicit values and meanings.

Current practice

We have noted that as far as Britain is concerned, we are describing potential rather than actuality. Empirical evidence (Byram and Risager, 1999) suggests that language teachers in England have not accepted the significance of the cultural dimension, even in the minimal form required in the National Curriculum.

On the other hand, where teachers are meeting with entirely new situations and responding to them in imaginative and open-minded ways, as is the case in Eastern and Central Europe in post-communist times, there are interesting examples of teachers giving full rein to the cultural dimension. For instance, one group of teachers adopted a comparative approach juxtaposing Russian and Irish identity. Their concern was to consider how 'we' are seen by 'others' rather than simply presenting 'others' (Byram and Tost Planet, 2000).

Some conclusions

It seems to us that the interaction of human rights education and foreign language-and-culture education can be enriching for both. The first can benefit from an emphasis on international interactions as part of human rights thinking, and the inter-lingual dimension which this necessarily requires. It is however not simply a matter of learning another language as if it were a transparent medium. Languages are heavily loaded with connotations from their use in different societies, and translation is, though not impossible, extremely difficult. This means then that interlingual communication is never as easy as many non-linguists assume.

Perhaps surprisingly, the same assumption – that at least in the early phases of language learning, there can be transparency – has also dominated the thinking of many language teachers in recent years. Language teachers have accepted the rhetoric of 'skills' and 'behavioural objectives' as they have struggled to make languages available to all potential learners. Therefore language teachers too need another perspective, as offered by human rights education, to re-assess their educational purposes as well as to recognise once more that human interaction is fundamental to their aims.

References

Audigier, F. (1998) *Basic Concepts and Core Competences of Education for Democratic Citizenship: an initial consolidated report.* [DECS/CIT (98) 35] Strasbourg: Council of Europe.

Brislin, R. and Yoshida, T. (1994) *Intercultural Communication Training: an introduction.* Thousand Oaks: Sage.

Byram, M. (1997) *Teaching and Assessing Intercultural Communicative Competence.* Clevedon: Multilingual Matters

Byram, M. and Risager, K. (1999) *Language Teachers, Politics and Cultures.* Clevedon: Multilingual Matters.

Byram, M. and/*et* Tost Planet, M. (Eds./Coord.) (2000) *Identité Sociale et Dimension Européenne. La Compétence Interculturelle par l'Apprentissage des Langues Vivantes. Social Identity and European Dimension. Intercultural Competence through Foreign Language Learning.* Graz: Council of Europe.

Byram, M. and Zarate, G. (1997) Definitions, objectives and assessment of sociocultural competence, in: M. Byram, G. Zarate and G. Neuner (eds.) *Sociocultural Competence in Language Learning and Teaching.* Strasbourg: Council of Europe.

Delors, J. (1996) *Learning: the treasure within. Report to UNESCO of the International Commission on Education for the Twenty-First Century.* Paris: UNESCO.

Doyé, P. (1993) Neuere konzepte der fremdsprachenerziehung und ihre bedeutung für die schulbuchkritik, in: M. Byram (ed.) *Germany: its representation in textbooks for teaching German in Great Britain.* Frankfurt/Main.

Figueroa, P. (2000) Citizenship education for a plural society in: A.Osler (ed.) *Citizenship and Democracy in Schools: diversity, identity, equality.* Stoke on Trent: Trentham.

Fraser, N. (1998) From redistribution to recognition? Dilemmas of justice in a 'post-socialist age', in C. Willet (ed.) *Theorizing Multiculturalism: a guide to current debate.* Malden, Ma.: Blackwell.

Giddens, A. (2000) Citizenship in the global era, in: N. Pearce and J. Hallgarten (eds.) *Tomorrow's Citizens: critical debates in citizenship and education.* London: Institute for Public Policy Research.

Guilherme, M. (2000) Critical Cultural Awareness: the critical dimension in foreign culture education. Unpublished PhD thesis, University of Durham.

Giroux, H. A. (1992) *Border Crossings: cultural workers and the politics of education.* New York: Routledge.

Habermas, J. (1979) *Communication and the Evolution of Society.* London: Heinemann.

Habermas, J. (1987) *The Philosophical Discourse of Modernity.* Cambridge, MA: The MIT Press.

Habermas, J. (1993) *Justification and Application.* Cambridge, Ma.: The MIT Press.

Hall, S. (2000) Multicultural citizens, monocultural citizenship? in: N. Pearce and J. Hallgarten (eds.) *Tomorrow's Citizens: critical debates in citizenship and education.* London: Institute for Public Policy Research.

Lyotard, J. F. (1986) *The Postmodern Condition: a report on knowledge.* Manchester: Manchester University Press.

Mendus, S. (1995) Toleration and recognition: education in a multicultural society. *Journal of Philosophy of Education* 29(2), 191-201.

Osler, A. and Starkey, H. (1996) *Teacher Education and Human Rights.* London: David Fulton.

Rassool, N. (1998) Postmodernity, cultural pluralism and the nation-state: problems of language rights, human rights, identity and power. *Language Sciences* 20(1), 89-99.

Starkey, H. (1996) Intercultural education through foreign language learning: a human rights approach, in: A.Osler, H.Rathenow, and H. Starkey (eds.) *Teaching for Citizenship in Europe.* Stoke on Trent: Trentham.

Wexler, P. (1993) Citizenship in the semiotic society, in: B. Turner (ed.) *Theories of Modernity and Postmodernity.* London: Sage.

Young, I. (1998) Polity and group difference: a critique of the ideal of universal citizenship, in: G. Shafir (ed.) *The Citizenship Debates.* Minneapolis: University of Minnesota Press.

6

Human Rights and Racial Justice: connections and contrasts

Robin Richardson

Famously, the great campaign for racial justice in the United States in the 1950s and 1960s was seen and experienced as a civil *rights* movement. In the 1990s, campaigns and laws in many Asian countries frequently operated with the concepts and legal framework of United Nations human rights standards. Do human rights also have the potential to focus work for racial justice in the United Kingdom? If so, what are the implications for education? These are the questions this chapter explores. It begins by stating the claim that human rights provide a convenient and powerful approach to dealing with issues of race and racism. It then recalls a range of objections, reservations and concerns. It ends by suggesting possible ways ahead. The chapter as a whole draws on deliberations in 1999 and 2000 in a project set up by the Runnymede Trust (Commission on the Future of Multi-Ethnic Britain, 2000).

The first great advantage claimed for human rights discourse is that it is comprehensive. It refers not only to 'first generation' rights (civil and political rights, stressing individual liberty and autonomy) but also to social and economic rights, and to rights relating to sustainable development and the environment. All rights – civil, political, economic, social and cultural – are seen as inter-related, and related also to development and democracy. In the words of the Vienna Declaration, agreed at the United Nations conference in

1993, democracy, development and respect for human rights and fundamental freedoms are interdependent and mutually reinforcing. In addition to non-discrimination provisions, there are obligations on governments to create the conditions necessary for the effective participation of persons belonging to national minorities in cultural, social and economic life and in public affairs. The discourse logically and inherently refers to responsibilities and obligations as well as to rights, since everyone has a duty to uphold and defend the rights of others. So in education, for example, it helps to stress that children and young people should be taught to take a stand against racist behaviour in the playground – they are to be more than mere bystanders.

Further, the story of international human rights is the story of argument and negotiation between largely autonomous cultures, traditions and states (Morsink, 1999). The actual realisation of human rights remains an ideal in all States, as does the universalisation of human rights in the world as a whole. It is also the case that most major documents run the risk of being bland and non-specific. Nevertheless real progress has been made in the international community over the last 50 years, and the negotiations, disputes and dialogues which have taken place in international arenas can act as models or paradigms for *intra*-national debates. Since the discourse is international it is neutral, in any one country, vis-à-vis the interests of specific communities or individuals. For example, *l'affaire des foulards* in France in the 1990s – the issue of whether school students should be allowed to wear *hijab* – was settled through reference to international human rights standards, not through distinctively French (or, for that matter, Islamic) law. Its international and cross-cultural character means also that struggles in different countries and situations can readily be compared and contrasted with each other, and can valuably learn from each other. It is particularly important that we in the UK should seek to learn from developments in other European countries.

Also, international human rights standards help to settle disputes within communities as well as between them, for example disputes between the generations and between the sexes, and between different lifestyles. Human rights discourse trumps, it is maintained, all other claims. They establish criteria for setting the limits of toleration, for example with regard to the customs and practices of a cultural group that are disputed by others. The Home Secretary has said of the Human Rights Act that it is

> ... an ethical language we can all recognise and sign up to. An ethical language which doesn't belong to any particular group or creed but to all of us. One that is based on principles of our common humanity'. (Straw, 1999)

It is relevant in this context to cite the present government's declaration that it is committed 'to creating One Nation', a country where

> every colour is a good colour ... every member of every part of society is able to fulfil their potential ... racism is unacceptable and counteracted ... everyone is treated according to their needs and rights ... everyone recognises their responsibilities ... racial diversity is celebrated'. (Home Office, 2000: 1)

Human rights discourse articulates the values and loyalties which must be shared by communities and individuals in One Nation. Even more importantly it provides a way of preventing One Nation from being oppressive and nationalistic. For it sets out ground rules for handling disputes and incompatible values between different communities and promotes public-spiritedness and willingness to compromise for the greater good.

Human rights discourse contributes to, and is fed by, a sense of global citizenship or a planetary ethos, as distinct from nationalism. It is therefore linked to the international rule of law and to policies (local, as in Local Agenda 21, as well as national and international) on sustainable development, and on addressing global inequalities between North and South. Further, it can unite people from different communities and heritages within the same nation state in what is sometimes known as 'constitutional patriotism'. Such patriotism is inherently internationalist and cosmopolitan.

A human rights framework helps to unite, both conceptually and on the ground (for example, in specific local authorities or organisations), struggles and discourses which might otherwise be in competition with each other and might indeed harm each other. By including race equality issues along with other equality issues, a human rights framework gives them a higher profile and shows them to be part and parcel of the overall system of justice. It thus prevents the possible marginalisation of antiracism, and prevents antiracism being seen as some sort of add-on option. For example, and particularly significantly, a human rights framework brings together race equality and gender equality. Struggles for race and gender equality can illuminate and strengthen each other. 'Races' and cultures are believed by racism to be fundamentally and essentially distinct from each other, as a matter of nature. Similarly sexism involves seeing all differences between women and men as fixed in nature rather than primarily constructed by culture. In both racism and sexism the dominant group holds much the same self/other stereotypes. The self (the male, the white person) is seen as rational, reliable, consistent, mature, capable, strong. The other is perceived and treated as emotional, untrustworthy, feckless, childish, wayward – a threat if not kept under strict control. A further interconnection derives from the fact that racism exacerbates, and is exacerbated by, sexism – often they reinforce each other in vicious circles and spirals, and intertwine to the extent that it is impossible to disentangle them. If such interconnections are not recognised it can happen – notoriously – that race equality initiatives benefit mainly Asian and black men, and that gender equality initiatives benefit mainly white women.

Human rights approaches provide an avenue to power for the disadvantaged, and are in this respect more robust than conventional politics, which is too often dominated by short-termism and considerations of electoral advantage. For human rights provide remedies which trump political powers. Also, non-governmental organisations (NGOs) have an established locus at international meetings and conferences, for example the United Nations Committee on the Elimination of Racism (CERD), and in consequence are able to exert additional pressure on the government of their own country.

Finally, there are certain pragmatic considerations. The present political context is one in which there is general acceptance of the notion of rights – the incorporation into UK law of the European Convention on Human Rights being one of the most salient features of this acceptance. It is in addition relevant to note that the development of a culture of rights is likely to be boosted and reinforced by devolution of powers from Westminster to Scotland and Wales, and by the creation of regional assemblies on the model developed first in Greater London.

The potential advantages of human rights theory, then, are substantial. However, the advantages will not be realised in theory unless major objections and challenges to the theory are rigorously examined. The challenges are partly theoretical and partly to do with how human rights are customarily talked about in practice. First, it is arguably disingenuous to maintain that human rights theory is neutral in relation to the interests of specific communities. For in the eighteenth century it was closely bound up with secularism, anti-clericalism and republicanism, and in the deliberations leading to the 1948 Universal Declaration the discourse was strongly affected by the experience of the 1939-45 war and by the early stages of the Cold War. The discourse can only be perceived as neutral if it is detached from the specific historical and cultural circumstances in which it was first fashioned and later developed.

The essential problem is that human rights theory tends, because of the historical contexts in which it was developed, to concentrate much more on the rights of individuals than on the rights of communities and that it tends to under-emphasise the importance – and indeed the inescapability – of culture. It is true that human rights discourse includes reference to culture, but typically it refers to recognition of 'minority' cultures rather than to the self-understanding of 'majority' cultures, and conceptualises cultures as static and sealed off from each other rather than as dynamic, developing and intermingling.

A further problem in relation to culture is that human rights discourse seems typically to envisage that human beings have rights by virtue of their humanity, as if humanity exists independently of culture. It is not in fact possible to imagine a human being independently of culture, however, for to be human is to have, or rather to belong to, a culture. Key issues, it follows, are how to understand culture and cultures; and how both to appreciate and to criticise cultural phenomena; and how to see both one's own culture and that of others as continually open to change, choice and development (Parekh, 2000). Human rights discourse is rather thin on such issues. In consequence it may serve the interests of older generations rather than younger, of religious leaders rather than secular, of conservative forces within a tradition rather than reformist, and of men rather than women.

Human rights champions maintain robustly that their discourse is comprehensive and that it refers not only the rights of individuals but also the rights of communities and groups to public recognition. There is a widespread perception, however, that these claims are not true in practice. On the contrary, there appears to be a hierarchy of rights, with 'fundamental' rights to do with liberty being seen as having a privileged status. The stress on 'Convention rights', following the incorporation of the European Convention on Human Rights into UK law, may well exacerbate this perception. The privileged status of civil rights ('first generation') seems to follow from the way in which the United Nations framework developed, for all too often economic and social rights look like additions or even afterthoughts.

Substantial gains have been made for race equality (as also for gender equality) over the years in Britain. These might be lost if the sharp focus on race equality were to be watered down by the less sharp and apparently more bland discourse of human rights. There are fears that specialist expertise built up since the Race Relations Act 1976 might be lost or dissipated; that campaigns and lobbies on race issues might be watered down; that the differences between various kinds of discrimination might be neglected and the distinctive mechanics and components of racism might be underplayed. In particular there appears a danger that a focus on human rights could dissipate energy away from responding to the challenges in the Stephen Lawrence Inquiry report. (Macpherson *et al,* 1999) The tabulation below lists the interacting components of institutional racism identified in the report and is based on a similar list in the report of the Commission on the Future of Multi-Ethnic Britain.

There is institutional racism in an organisation, for example a school, a local education authority or a country's educational system, if:

- members of Asian and black communities do not receive their fair share of the benefits and resources available from organisations, and do not receive a professional, responsive and high-quality service

- they do, however, receive more than their fair share of penalties and disadvantages

- members of Asian and black communities are not recruited to the extent that could reasonably be expected, or, having been recruited, receive less than their fair share of promotion, training and career development opportunities

- racist arguments, stereotypes and assumptions go unchallenged in everyday conversation and affect how the organisation treats members of the public

- there is cynicism about so-called political correctness in staff culture, and little or no reference to issues connected with reducing inequalities and valuing diversity

- Asian and black staff feel that they do not really belong in the culture of the workplace, for their world-views, cultures and experiences of racism are not acknowledged

- senior management positions are disproportionately held by white people

- few or no efforts have been made to recruit Asian and black people to senior positions or to involve them in major decision-making

- the task of addressing institutional racism is not regarded as a high priority for leaders and managers, either personally or professionally, and is seldom or never considered in mainstream decision-making;

- few members of an organisation's staff have skills in inter-cultural understanding and communication, and in handling and defusing situations of actual or potential conflict and tension

- few staff have received relevant high-quality training, and few therefore understand the concept of institutional racism, and do not know what they themselves can do to address it

- the organisation does not listen to, let alone seek out, the views and perceptions of Asian and black people

- the organisation does not systematically examine the impact of their policies and practices in order to judge whether or not it has a negative impact on Asian and black com-munities.

It is relevant and sobering in this context to recall that hitherto in Britain human rights discourse has paid very little attention to issues of racial justice, for example to the organisational issues listed above. Further there is not a strong sense of struggle and large-scale mobilisation, as for example there was in the United States civil rights movement, or recently in Britain in relation to the Stephen Lawrence Inquiry. In so far as human rights feature in the popular media, the reference has typically been to issues in distant countries, particularly in the former colonies of European powers, and has seemed to involve lecturing such countries about their backward-ness. The sub-text, typically, is that they are not living up to Euro-pean standards and were better off under colonialism. It is forgotten in such lectures that – for example – there are higher levels on incarceration in the United States than in almost any other country in the world, and that African Americans are disproportionately affected by this.

In the light of the debates and disagreements recalled above, four broad principles may be identified to guide future developments in education. First, an apparently trivial semantic point which is in reality of considerable importance: it is frequently appropriate to engage in what is sometimes called 'the politics of conjunctions' –'human rights *and* cultural identity', 'human rights *and* racial justice', and so on. To recall a well-known metaphor, human rights theory is one leg of a three-legged stool. It cannot be expected to bear the whole weight. There are important implications from this simple point for curriculum planning and also for school organisation (Carolan, this volume).

Second, it is essential to stress concepts of political debate and deliberative democracy: the right (or need) for as many people as possible to be involved in debates and deliberations about the good society, particularly the multi-ethnic or multicultural good society. Pupils and students in schools need to engage in grassroots intercultural conversation, in order to interpret the various human rights documents and to ground them in lived experience and struggle. Without such conversations and deliberations the documents will for most people remain, as the term sometimes is, 'letters to Father Christmas'. The conversations must be not only intercultural, of course, but also must ensure that women's voices are heard at least as strongly as men's.

Third, it is important to bear always in mind that a major reason why race equality discourse has wide currency is that it has developed out of struggle, and derives strength from a body of narrative – the story of antiracism and emancipation over several centuries and in many lands, vivid in many specific contexts and lived out and inspired by many specific campaigns, heroes and heroines. If human rights discourse is to gain similar currency there will need to be an analogous sense of struggle and an analogous body of narrative, story and specificity. The United States civil rights movement, in this respect, is a valuable model, for it involved thousands of ordinary people and organisations, not just a few exceptional leaders, and used a wide range of strategies. It influenced, and was influenced by, other social and liberation movements and developed its own culture. The *Homebeats* material developed by the Institute of Race Relations shows vividly that there are many stories to research and teach about in Britain (Institute of Race Relations, new edition 1999. See also Phillips and Phillips, 1998).

Fourth, educators need to develop the notions of 'white ally' and 'moral co-equal' (Blum, 1999). In the United States, white people were involved in the Civil Rights Movement and the Underground Railroad and were active in South Africa in the fight against apartheid. Similar images or icons of white people working as allies need to be developed in educational materials in Britain. All too often white people have only three main models of whiteness available to them: (a) white supremacism (b) denial and indifference (c) guilt. The notion of white ally is a fourth possibility (Tatum, 1994). It is important to go beyond this notion, however, to that of comrade or of equal partner. Comradeship develops in and through shared struggle. Two tenants' organisations on an estate in east London recently had to go into alliance with each other to create a Tenant Management Co-operative to gain access to much-needed capital funds. The one organisation was wholly white and the other wholly Bangladeshi. It was subsequently reported that 'racial harassment on the estate is now virtually non-existent and although the two communities may not exactly be in each other's arms all the time, they cohabit the same space in a friendly and peaceful fashion' (Sibbit, 1997). Many such stories of comradeship, and of cohabitation of the same space in a friendly and peaceful fashion, are required.

The first draft outlines of the Universal Declaration of Human Rights were prepared by one John P. Humphrey, who in 1947 was the newly appointed director of the UN Secretariat's division on human rights. On Sunday 17 February 1947 he was invited by Eleanor Roosevelt, who was chair of the Commission on Human Rights which the UN had set up, to visit her at her Washington Square apartment in New York. Also present were the vice-chair of the Commission, Peng-Chun Chang of China, and the rapporteur, Charles Habib Malik of Lebanon. It was at this meeting that Humphrey was asked to start drafting. Many years later he recalled the meeting as follows (Humphrey, 1984, quoted in Morsink, 1999: 5):

> Chang and Malik were too far apart in their philosophical approaches to be able to work together on a text. There was a good deal of talk but we were getting nowhere. Then, after another cup of tea, Chang suggested that I put my other duties aside for six months and study Chinese philosophy, after which I might be able to prepare a text for the committee. This was his way of saying that Western influences might be too great, and he was looking at Malik as he spoke. He had already, in the Commission,

urged the importance of historical perspective. There was some more discussion mainly of a philosophical character, Mrs Roosevelt saying little and continuing to pour tea.

It is a beautiful vignette of people dwelling 'in the same space in a friendly and peaceful fashion'. If human rights and racial justice are to dwell together, so also must philosophy and the pouring of tea, public ceremony and private courtesy, grandness and homeliness, the sweep of history and the specificity of the present moment. The challenge is enormous. But schools and school classrooms, it cannot be doubted, have essential and invaluable roles to play.

References

Blum, L. (1999) Race, community and moral education: Kohlberg and Spielberg as civic educators. *Journal of Moral Education*, 28 (2) 125-44.

Carolan, S. (2000) Parents, human rights and racial justice, in A. Osler (ed.) *Citizenship and Democracy in Schools: diversity, identity, equality*. Stoke on Trent: Trentham.

Commission on the Future of Multi-Ethnic Britain (2000) *The Future of Multi-Ethnic Britain*. London: Profile Books.

Habermas, J. (1993) Struggles for recognition in Constitutional States, *European Journal of Philosophy*, 1 (2).

Home Office (2000), *Race Equality and Public Services*. London: The Stationery Office.

Humphreys, J. (1984) *Human Rights and the United Nations: a great adventure*. Dobbs Ferry, New York: Transnational.

Institute of Race Relations (1999) *Homebeats* (CD ROM), London: Institute of Race Relations.

Macpherson, W. *et al* (1999) *The Stephen Lawrence Inquiry: report of an inquiry by Sir William Macpherson of Cluny*. London: The Stationery Office.

Morsink, J. (1999) *The Universal Declaration of Human Rights: origins, drafting and intent*. Philadelphia: University of Pennsylvania Press.

Parekh, B. (2000) *Rethinking Multiculturalism: cultural diversity and political theory*. Basingstoke: Macmillan.

Phillips, M. and Phillips, T. (1998) *Windrush: the irresistible rise of multiracial Britain*. London: Harper Collins.

Sibbit, R. (1997) *The Perpetrators of Racial Violence and Racial Harassment*. London: The Stationery Office.

Straw, J. (1999) *Building on a Human Rights Culture*. The Home Secretary's address to Civil Service College Seminar, 9 December.

Tatum, B. (1997) *Why Are All the Black Kids Sitting Together in the Cafeteria?* New York: Basic Books.

7

Human Rights, Responsibilities and School Self-Evaluation

Audrey Osler and Hugh Starkey

The United Nations has declared 1995-2004 the decade for human rights education and the Council of Europe has recognised such education as a priority since 1978. The results of the work of these organisations and of non-governmental organisations (NGOs) working in this field have been widely disseminated internationally and have had an impact in Britain on the programmes of study and the guidance for Citizenship (Starkey, 1991; Osler and Starkey, 1996; Osler, 1998, 2000b). In many respects the content and pedagogy associated with human rights education is well developed and supported by policy statements and internationally agreed texts. However, the notion of human responsibilities, which is commonly collocated with human rights, is less obviously agreed and defined. This chapter discusses the concept of internationally agreed rights and responsibilities and considers their implications for education.

Legal steps towards a human rights culture

Within Western European democracies, the term human rights is often linked in the media and thus in the public mind to such violations of civic and political rights as those exposed by Amnesty International or Human Rights Watch. In reality, a recognition of human rights is a pre-requisite for any social interaction that is not subject to the pressures of abusive or arbitrary force. This understanding of human rights, namely that human relationships should be conducted on the basis of equality of respect and dignity, is universally accepted, in principle at least. Any negotiation with respect to business or to daily life depends on an acceptance of the rule of law and the renouncing of violence and coercion as means to an end. Behaviour which flouts these principles is likely to be stigmatised as unacceptable or, indeed, criminal.

At the World Conference on Human Rights in Vienna in 1993, 171 states, representing 98 per cent of the world's population, signed a Declaration and Programme of Action which re-affirmed in Article 1:

> the solemn commitment of all States to fulfil their obligations to promote universal respect for, and observance and protection of, all human rights and fundamental freedoms for all in accordance with the Charter of the United Nations, other instruments relating to human rights, and international law. The universal nature of these rights and freedoms is beyond question. (UNHCR, 1994)

The United Nations is thus able to claim legitimately that the rights embedded in the Universal Declaration of Human Rights

> ...have gained prominence as a universally recognised set of norms and standards that increasingly inform all aspects of our relations as individuals and as collective members of groups, within communities and among nations. There is now near-universal recognition that respect for human rights – the rights of political choice and association, of opinion and expression, and of culture; the freedom from fear and from all forms of discrimination and prejudice; freedom from want and the right to employment and well-being and, collectively, to development – is essential to the sustainable achievement of the three agreed global priorities of peace, development and democracy. (United Nations, 1998)

The above quotation defines the scope of human rights to include culture and, by implication, education. It also sets out the three global priorities of *peace, development* and *democracy*. These three global priorities reflect a gradual evolution of the international agenda since the formation of the United Nations in 1945. The goals of the UN as set out in its Charter are *peace*, or at least saving 'succeeding generations from the scourge of war'; justice and respect for international law; 'social progress and better standards of life in larger freedom'. In 1969 the UN General Assembly proclaimed a Declaration on Social Progress and Development.

By 1986, with the adoption of the Declaration on the Right to Development, there was full recognition within the UN community that *development* was the term to describe this third element relating to 'social progress and better standards of life in larger freedom'. Such development was now explicitly defined as a right. At the Vienna conference of 1993 this right was reaffirmed and linked to *democracy* as the expression of the concept most likely to ensure the second goal of the UN Charter, namely, justice and respect for international law. Thus peace, development and democracy, which require a commitment to human rights by States and an understanding of human rights by individuals, are the current expression of universal goals. This is well expressed in the Vienna Declaration:

> The efforts of the United Nations system towards the universal respect for, and observance of, human rights and fundamental freedoms for all, contribute to the stability and well-being necessary for peaceful and friendly relations among nations, and to improved conditions for peace and security as well as social and economic development, in conformity with the Charter of the United Nations. (Article 6)

> Democracy, development and respect for human rights and fundamental freedoms are interdependent and mutually reinforcing. Democracy is based on the freely expressed will of the people to determine their own political, economic, social and cultural systems and their full participation in all aspects of their lives. In the context of the above, the promotion and protection of human rights and fundamental freedoms at the national and international levels should be universal and conducted without conditions attached. The international community should support the strengthening and promoting of democracy, development and respect for human rights and fundamental freedoms in the entire world. (Article 8)

For the achievement of peace, development and democracy, a culture of human rights is necessary. This was expressed by one of the architects of the Universal Declaration, René Cassin in an address to teachers:

> When [teachers] teach about human rights, when they convey to their pupils the notion of their rights, their dignity and their duties as citizens and human beings, then they are carrying out a task that complements wonderfully the work that we have achieved at the highest level...

> Legal force of itself is only a secondary safety valve: it is the education of young people and even of adults that constitutes the primary and real

guarantee for minority groups faced with racial hatred that leads so easily to violence and murder. (Alliance Israélite Universelle, 1961:123, *our translation*)

Cassin's argument is twofold. First, rights are only meaningful when people know about them and understand them. Secondly, it is the culture of a society more than the law itself that creates the conditions for democracy and for social peace. The law, of course, contributes in its turn to the creation of such a culture. For example, in Britain, anti-discriminatory legislation, notably the 1976 Race Relations Act, which outlawed both direct and indirect racial discrimination and gave powers to a new Commission for Racial Equality, have contributed to a social climate of improved race relations (Parekh, 1991; Blackstone, Parekh and Sanders, 1998). Despite limitations and flaws, the law has enabled a climate to develop over the past 25 years in which direct discrimination and overt manifestations of racism are no longer a regular feature of daily life.

Education and a global culture of human rights

The Director General of UNESCO, Koichiro Matsuura points out the dual potential of education:

We have to note that, unfortunately, education has not always and in all circumstances, served to liberate peoples from the barriers of ignorance. It hasn't always helped them to affirm their dignity nor to map their own destiny freely. It has also served, and continues to do so, to bolster ruling elites, to exclude and even, it has to be said, to ferment conflicts. And this is precisely because education is not just a means of acquiring knowledge, but also a vehicle for moral and ideological training available to any social organisation. (*Le Monde*, 20 April, 2000, *our translation*)

Matsuura poses the question as to whether education in the spirit of the United Nations is compatible with equally powerful claims to the freedom for communities to determine their own culture. It is often women and girls whose human rights are denied when claims to cultural specificity outside the frame of reference provided by international standards are pursued. They may be denied access to education or to the best quality education available, particularly when resources are limited. Other discriminatory practices operating within schools, such as low expectations of female students and the use of textbooks which reinforce gender stereotyping, are sometimes justified as being in keeping with community norms and cultural practices. In such contexts the universality of human rights is called into question. Matsuura responds by reaffirming this universality:

> In spite of the vast number of systems of values, surely a common corpus of values is acknowledged in the Universal Declaration of Human Rights? The respect of this text by all human communities will in any case determine whether humanity can control its own destiny. And this is precisely the crusade being undertaken by UNESCO. (*ibid.*)

The creation of a global culture of human rights appears to be the only means by which the universal goals of peace, development and democracy can be achieved. Other radical solutions, such as state socialism, have been tried but have failed to deliver both development and freedoms. Education has a crucial role in promoting such a culture. In turn, a culture of human rights has profound implications for educational structures and priorities.

The concern to promote a global culture of human rights is international, but it is equally relevant and applicable at national and at local level. For example, within the UK, the Government has promoted a discourse of a 'culture of rights', based on a 'shared understanding'. Within this discourse rights are 'balanced' by the responsibilities and duties of citizens:

> The Human Rights Act is fundamentally about modernising our society and building a new culture of rights balanced by responsibilities within UK law. Rights and responsibilities go together. They are two sides of the same coin. The new culture that we want to build is one in which the Human Rights Act gives us a shared understanding of what is fundamentally right and wrong, a culture where people recognise the duties that citizens owe to each other and the wider community and are willing to fulfil them – and one in which public authorities understand that the Human Rights Act defines what the basic rights are. It will sometimes require us to be robust about an individual's rights if we are to maintain the rights of others. That is the culture that we want to build. That is what the Human Rights Act is all about. (Lord Bassam, Home Office Minister, Hansard, 10 Jan 2000: Columns 481-2)

Whilst the building of such a culture at national level can be the responsibility of both government and NGOs, the building of such a culture in microcosm, at school level, is a legitimate goal for head-teachers and school governing bodies. We explore below ways in which this culture can be promoted and the benefits to schools of adopting such an approach. However, first we note a particular threat to this culture.

Racism: threatening the culture of human rights

In May 2000, as part of the United Nations programme in its Third Decade to Combat Racism and Racial Discrimination, a preparatory conference was held in advance of the World Conference Against Racism, South Africa, 2001. The focus of the Third Decade is based on the recognition that every society in the world is affected and hindered by discrimination. Prevention through education, parti-cularly human rights education, is seen as pivotal in order to look at the roots of racism and make institutional changes in order to prevent its eruption.

Looking ahead to the conference and the preparatory meetings in her message on International Human Rights Day in 1999, the UN High Commissioner for Human Rights, Mary Robinson stressed the threat of racism to a global culture of human rights:

> Racism and xenophobia are powerful causes of conflict; in fact, if you look closely at the roots of history's most violent confrontations, you will see their malign influence at work. And they are found everywhere. No society is free from at least some people who are intolerant of difference, whether ethnic or religious, and whose intolerance finds violent expression. (UN press release HR/99/115, 10 December, 1999 www.unhchr.ch).

The crucial importance of education as a means to tackle the roots of racism is also stressed by Matsuura. He notes the tension between the unifying forces of globalisation and the need for communities to assert their rights to cultural diversity. Such assertions, when coupled with a refusal to respect the rights of others, are the basis of the most serious conflicts currently pre-occupying the world community:

> Individuals and communities need to harness the potential of culture to ensure that globalisation and the consequent homogenisation of knowledge is counterbalanced by the preservation of cultural diversity and

individual identities. [...] Each society and each citizen needs the values and skills to counter intolerance and conflict at the root. (Koichiro Matsuura, UNESCO press release, 15 February, 2000 *www.unesco.org*).

The contribution of citizenship education

The role of education for citizenship in helping young people to acquire 'the values and skills to counter intolerance' is seen as crucial in most democratic societies. In France, for instance, the programmes of study for the lower secondary school define the purpose of this stage of schooling as to provide an education

> ...for human rights and citizenship, through the acquisition of the principles and the values which underpin and organise democracy and the Republic, through knowledge of institutions and laws, through an understanding of the rules of social and political life. (Ministère de l'Éducation Nationale 1998: 36 *our translation*).

The equivalent statement in a British context is the second aim of the revised National Curriculum for England. While this statement can be interpreted as supporting education for human rights, it avoids any direct or explicit reference to human rights or human rights education. Indeed the term rights is used in a restricted sense to refer to consumer rights:

> It should develop [pupils'] knowledge, understanding and appreciation of their own and different beliefs and cultures, and how these influence individuals and societies. The school curriculum should pass on enduring values, develop pupils' integrity and autonomy and help them to be responsible and caring citizens capable of contributing to the development of a just society. It should promote equal opportunities and enable pupils to challenge discrimination and stereotyping. It should develop their awareness and understanding of, and respect for, the environments in which they live, and secure their commitment to sustainable development at a personal, local, national and global level. It should also equip pupils as consumers to make informed judgements and independent decisions and to understand their responsibilities and rights. (QCA, 1999)

Certainly there is a commitment to promoting an 'appreciation of their own and different beliefs and cultures', to 'the development of a just society', to equal opportunities and challenging 'discrimination and stereotyping' and to 'sustainable development'. This might be summarised as an education for the three UN priorities of peace, development and democracy, although only one of these three terms is actually used.

Creating a culture of human rights in schools is a project that will contribute to peace and justice globally. The introduction of Citizenship into the national curriculum in England in 2000 provides an opportunity to include knowledge of human rights in the programme of study of all children, in accordance with Article 26 of the Universal Declaration. However, the inclusion of human rights in a programme of study is no guarantee that such teaching will be well received. The culture of the school needs itself to be based on a culture of human rights for such education to be credible and effective.

Evaluating the culture of human rights in schools

Inspection is one means by which standards in schools are assessed. In England the inspection agency, OFSTED, is required to report on how well the school cares for its pupils, the quality of the curriculum opportunities offered, and the extent to which equal opportunities and inclusion prevail in a school. However, such inspections provide a snapshot view at a particular moment in a school's development and they rely to a considerable extent on what can be seen and measured. Inspection can contribute to the monitoring of equality initiatives, although its effectiveness is likely to depend on effective leadership, and the awareness, commitment and training of inspection teams (Osler and Morrison, 2000). Schools need also to engage in a continuous process of self-evaluation and a number of instruments have been developed to help schools in this respect.

Given the importance of the United Nations Convention on the Rights of the Child (1989), which is by far the most widely ratified human rights convention, and given its particular relevance for schools, we have developed an instrument entitled: *Does your school environment give everyone a chance to enjoy their rights?* (Osler and Starkey, 1998). Pupils, teachers, heads, parents, governors are provided with 23 statements and invited to respond by 'always', 'sometimes' or 'never'. These are statements arranged in three sections according to their relevance to the three broad themes of the Convention, namely provision, protection and participation. Each statement is followed by a list of the main articles of the Convention to which it relates. For example:

> (Provision) In the teaching of national history, due weight is given to women and minorities and to their versions of history (Articles 2, 13, 28, 29.1c and d, 30).

> (Protection) A student accused of breaking the rules is presumed innocent until proven guilty and carries on with classes (Article 28.2, 40).

> (Participation) Students and adults (including parents, teachers and administrative staff) are consulted about the quality of the teaching in the school (Article 5, 12, 18).

The questionnaire also draws on descriptions of pedagogic principles derived from the Convention (Osler and Starkey, 1996: 153-6). A similar instrument, but based on the Universal Declaration of Human Rights, can be found in Shiman (1999). Both these questionnaires are draft instruments which can be adapted by schools for their own use. They are indicative of an approach to school self-evaluation within a human rights framework. We see them as contributing to the development of a culture of self-evaluation for human rights rather than as providing definitive measures. Since it is often also difficult for inspectors to assess the human rights culture of a school, it is important that teachers feel confident in a developing their own methods of self-evaluation, which may form the basis of a discussion of such issues with external assessors such as school inspectors.

Identifying responsibilities

Article 29 of the Universal Declaration states that: 'Everyone has duties to the community in which alone the free and full development of his personality is possible'.

This explicit reference to duties, or what are now more usually referred to as responsibilities, as an essential element of a human rights framework has received relatively little attention in liberal democracies. Whereas it took three years, between the signing of the United Nations Charter and the final adoption of the Universal Declaration, to define human rights to the satisfaction of all parties, no such attempt was made to define human responsibilities.

René Cassin attempted, in 1947, to include a formulation of duties in the Universal Declaration. However, Eleanor Roosevelt argued that the principles of individual liberty, which had driven the war against nazism and fascism, were over-riding. It was agreed to leave the formulation of duties until after the completion of the formulation of rights, but no commission was ever convened to undertake this task (Cassin, 1969). As we have noted above, much current discourse of human rights brackets responsibilities with rights. The prime architect of the 'Third Way' goes so far as to propose the maxim 'no rights without responsibilities' (Giddens, 1998:66).

It is possible to derive responsibilities from rights, but in attempting to arrive at a definition in this way, it becomes clear that there is not a straightforward one-to-one equivalence between rights and responsibilities. It is therefore most important to be able to obtain agreement on a definition of the concept, as has been achieved for the concept of rights. Indeed in May 1999, the Committee of Ministers of Education of the Council of Europe adopted a Declaration and Programme on Education for Democratic Citizenship, based on the rights and responsibilities of citizens (Council of Europe, 1999a) which will attempt to define this relationship in the context of education. The key issues to be pursued under this programme include:

> the relationships between rights and responsibilities as well as common responsibilities in combating social exclusion, marginalisation, civic apathy, intolerance and violence.

We might expect that the Committee will review existing definitions of responsibilities in current human rights instruments and will explore their meaning.

The first attempt to define responsibilities in a human rights instrument is contained in the African Charter on Human and Peoples' Rights, adopted in 1981 by the Member States of the Organisation of African Unity. The Charter includes defined duties and responsibilities. Article 25 places an obligation upon States to promote education for the rights in the Charter and to 'see to it that these freedoms and rights as well as corresponding obligations and duties are understood'.

There follows a section (Articles 27–29) defining the duties and responsibilities of individuals, as opposed to those of States and of parents.

Article 27
1. Every individual shall have duties towards his family and society, the State and other legally recognised communities and the international community.

2. The rights and freedoms of each individual shall be exercised with due regard to the rights of others, collective security, morality and common interest.

Article 28
Every individual shall have the duty to respect and consider his fellow beings without discrimination, and to maintain relations aimed at promoting, safeguarding and reinforcing mutual respect and tolerance.

Article 29
The individual shall also have the duty:

1. To preserve the harmonious development of the family and to work for the cohesion and respect of the family; to respect his parents at all times, to maintain them in case of need;

2. To serve his national community by placing his physical and intellectual abilities at its service;

3. Not to compromise the security of the State whose national or resident he is;

4. To preserve and strengthen social and national solidarity, particularly when the latter is threatened;

5. To preserve and strengthen the national independence and the territorial integrity of his country and to contribute to its defence in accordance with the law;

6. To work to the best of his abilities and competence, and to pay taxes imposed by law in the interest of the society;

7. To preserve and strengthen positive African cultural values in his relation with other members of the society, in the spirit of tolerance, dialogue and consultation and, in general, to contribute to the promotion of the moral well-being of society;

8. To contribute to the best of his abilities, at all times and at all levels, to the promotion and achievement of African unity.

Whilst the above definitions have a distinctively African flavour, an attempt to define a list of universal responsibilities was made by the Commission for Global Governance, in its report published at the time of the fiftieth anniversary of the United Nations (Commission on Global Governance, 1995). The impetus for setting up the Commission came from Willy Brandt soon after the fall of the Berlin Wall in 1989. It was subsequently endorsed by the then Secretary General of the United Nations, Boutros Boutros-Ghali. The Commission, chaired by Shridath Ramphal of Guyana and Ingvar Carlsson of Sweden, included members from nearly 30 countries, broadly representative of the world community.

The Commission distilled from all the human rights instruments available, a list of eight fundamental universal rights and seven universal responsibilities. The list of responsibilities is as follows:

- contribute to the common good

- consider the impact of their actions on the security and welfare of others

- promote equity, including gender equity

- protect the interests of future generations by pursuing sustainable development and safeguarding the global commons

- preserve humanity's cultural and intellectual heritage

- be active participants in governance

- work to eliminate corruption

Although the form in which these responsibilities is expressed varies from the African Charter, it broadly echoes its intentions, while attempting to provide explicit but concise formulations. The seventh responsibility, the elimination of corruption, is innovative in human rights discourse. It is not hard to justify, however, as corruption is corrosive of democracy – the main guarantee of justice, equality and sustainable development.

A third document which goes some way to defining responsibilities is another regional instrument, this time developed by the Council of

Europe. In 1999 the Parliamentary Assembly adopted a Recommendation (1401) *Education in the responsibilities of the individual.* Drawing on expressions of fundamental values, particularly as expressed in the European Convention on Human Rights, the Universal Declaration of Human Rights, the European Social Charter and the Framework Convention for the Protection of National Minorities, the Assembly concludes that:

> Everyone should, *inter alia*:
>
> a. fully respect the dignity, value and freedom of other people, without distinction of race, religion, sex, nationality, ethnic origin, social status, political opinion, language or age; everyone must act towards others in a spirit of fellowship and tolerance;
>
> b. act peacefully without recourse to physical violence or mental pressure;
>
> c. respect the opinions, privacy and personal and family life of other people;
>
> d. show solidarity and stand up for the rights of others;
>
> e. in practising his or her own religion, respect other religions, without fomenting hatred or advocating fanaticism, but rather promoting general mutual tolerance;
>
> f. respect the environment and use energy resources with moderation, giving thought to the well-being of future generations.

It would appear that the European formulation was produced in ignorance of the seven responsibilities identified by the Commission for Global Governance. Given the cultural mandate of the Council of Europe, a reference to the preservation of cultural heritage would be logical. Similarly, given its mission to promote democracy, the failure to highlight active participation appears an oversight.

An audit of responsibilities

Both the African Charter and the Parliamentary Assembly of the Council of Europe identify responsibilities which are not found in the report of the Commission on Global Governance. However, the clarity of the Commission's conclusions and its claim to universality leads us to focus on these rather than on the regional instruments. We suggest that the seven responsibilities have implications for schools, which we see as a forming a minimal requirement. In particular,

young people should learn about their responsibilities and the implications of these for their behaviour and life-style. The provenance
of this formulation of universal responsibilities should ensure the
possibility of acknowledgement of its legitimacy in multi-faith and
multi-ethnic communities. In the context of education for citizenship, and in addressing Personal, Social and Health Education,
schools should provide opportunities for pupils and teaching staff
and other stakeholders to consider the following as both individual
and shared responsibilities.

Contribute to the common good

This active obligation to work to further the aims of the community
supposes that the aims are made known and that they are shared, that
is that each member of the community feels ownership of the goals
of the institution. The aims will need to be re-visited periodically to
take into account changing circumstances and changing cohorts of
students and to enable new members of the community to contribute
to the process of reformulation. There are many ways in which
institutions can initiate their members and retain their loyalty to the
common purpose. In some cases this will include an identification
of institutional goals and some form of shared acknowledgement of
symbols. These may take many different forms: they might include
school assemblies, a school song, celebration or prize-giving or
perhaps the wearing of a uniform or badge. Provided that the cere-
monies or rituals are based on human rights principles and inclusive
of all, it can be expected that all members of the school will be able
to support the aims expressed. All activity in the school should then
be directed to achieving the aims and thus contribute to the common
good. However, ceremonial expression of common loyalties needs to
be matched by real opportunities for sharing in the benefits provided
by the institution.

Consider the impact of their actions on the security and welfare of others

This obligation follows from the previous one. When many people
interact in close physical proximity, as in schools, these considerations are particularly important. Although individuals have the res-

ponsibility to be considerate, the institution is greatly helped when approved practices and procedures are formalised. For instance, something as simple as keeping to the left on stairs or not running in corridors will contribute greatly to physical security and welfare. Moreover, psychological security is equally important. Students and staff need to work together to develop policies and practices which enable all individuals to feel safe from ridicule and harassment.

Promote equity, including gender equity

In view of the right to equitable treatment, the institution is obligated to have policies that help to ensure equity. At the same time individuals have the responsibility to do their best to promote the policies. At a minimum, that implies that both staff and students are familiar with equal opportunities issues and the policies that derive from them. Ideally, both staff and students should be involved in the formulation of such policies and all parties or their representatives should be involved in the design and monitoring of such policies. They should cover the curriculum as well as the informal provisions of the school and its ethos. Gender equity should not be divorced from other equality issues such as those relating to race and disability.

Protect the interests of future generations by pursuing sustainable development and safeguarding the global commons

All members of the institution will be committed to preserving its assets and protecting communal facilities. They will also have an education that helps them acquire a global perspective and an understanding of the concept of sustainable development. Schools will provide opportunities for pupils to become familiar with local Agenda 21 initiatives. The publication, *A Curriculum for Global Citizenship* (Oxfam, 1997) provides detailed guidance and resources across the whole age-range.

Preserve humanity's cultural and intellectual heritage

Traditionally this has been a major function of schools and universities. The reference is to the heritage of humanity rather than of single nations or regions. This implies a broadly based curriculum, again with a global perspective. For example, in the teaching of history no one national or religious perspective should be adopted. Students should be encouraged to understand that historical events are interpreted from a variety of perspectives in different times and places.

Be active participants in governance

Institutions are obligated to provide structures for participation. Individuals have a responsibility to be involved. Involvement can take many forms – at its most basic may simply imply voting for a representative. The school has a responsibility to establish participative structures, such as school or class councils, and students should be encouraged to consider issues and decisions which affect them. Such structures might share responsibility for the allocation of resources.

Work to eliminate corruption

Most schools are financed with public funds and those ultimately responsible for the institution must be accountable for the use of those funds. Democracy implies transparency in the use of resources and any use of the funds for purposes incompatible with the goals of the institution may be considered corrupt. All members of the institution – staff and students – should be aware of the possibility of corruption and know what steps are open to them if corruption is suspected. As with issues of security, measures of prevention should be in place. It is likely that work to eliminate corruption will be collective, perhaps involving unions or associations of parents, for example.

Children's own understandings of rights, responsibilities and participation

It is sometimes argued that, if informed about their rights, young people will begin to demand rights without acknowledging their responsibilities. Moreover, it is sometimes asserted that young people do not want responsibilities, and that they see these as the preserve of adults. Not only is this a fundamental misunderstanding of the nature of children's human rights, which are based on the principle of reciprocity, that is to say, respecting and upholding the rights of others (see for example, Osler and Starkey, 1996 and 1998; Flekkøy and Kaufman, 1997) but it is also, perhaps, to underestimate young people's capacity and willingness to acknowledge their responsibilities.

In a research project conducted on behalf of the UK Commission for Racial Equality into exclusion from school (Osler, 1997), young people were invited to give their opinions on improving school discipline. They acknowledged that they shared a responsibility with teachers for ensuring that the school was an orderly place where everyone had an opportunity to learn, and were eager to develop their own skills and capacities to resolve conflicts and to participate more fully in decision-making processes. Their consultation and involvement in our research, which set out to identify good practice in managing school discipline and minimising school exclusions, produced a wealth of creative ideas which complemented those of their teachers and gave us new insights. In particular, pupils highlight that if schools are to ensure the greater participation of young people in decision-making in line with the provisions of the Convention on the Rights of the Child, schools must not only provide structures for participation (school councils, class councils etc.) but also equip children with the skills to participate (e.g. advocacy, counselling and listening skills, conflict resolution). Pupils saw structured opportunities for exercising their participation rights as a fundamental part of a well-disciplined school (Osler, 2000a).

Conclusion

The twenty-first century world is a global village within which diverse traditions and cultures co-exist and interact. This is a source of rich creativity, but also potentially a source of tensions and conflicts. Schools, particularly those in cities, are often microcosms, reflecting the global diversity of populations. Even when schools are more homogenous in their composition, they have to prepare their pupils to live and work in a heterogeneous world. For all these reasons education is crucially about helping young citizens to develop those values and skills that will help them contribute to the global priorities of peace, sustainable development and the means to achieve these, namely democracy and respect for human rights.

Individuals have rights. In addition institutions and individuals have responsibilities. In the case of education, those involved as students, teachers or in support roles are expected to be aware of the key principles and guidelines set out in Article 26.2 of the Universal Declaration of Human Rights. The study of this and the full text of the Universal Declaration can inspire local statements of values, such as those contained in school mission statements and policy documents.

Much work has been done on the application of human rights values to education. There is a developing rhetoric stressing the essential reciprocity of rights and responsibilities. It is relatively easy to convince individuals that they have rights, since rights are strong claims that they can make in the expectation that they will receive benefits such as protection and the provision of services. Responsibilities, on the other hand, imply not receiving but giving; not individualism but a sense of the communal and the collective. This has been and continues to be a feature of many religious traditions and values. In an increasingly secular context, there is a continuing pedagogical challenge, namely to promote responsibilities linked to rights for the achievement of global priorities.

References

Alliance Israélite Universelle (1961) *Les Droits de l'Homme et L'Éducation.* Paris: Presses Universitaires de France.

Blackstone, T., Parekh, B. and Sanders, P. (eds.) (1998) *Race Relations in Britain : a developing agenda.* London: Routledge.

Cassin, R. (1969) *From the Ten Commandments to the Rights of Man* (original source unknown) published at *www.udhr50/org/history/tencomms.htm.*

Commission On Global Governance (1995) *Our Global Neighbourhood.* Oxford: Oxford University Press.

Council of Europe (1999a) Committee of Ministers of Education *Declaration and Programme on Education for Democratic Citizenship, Based on the Rights and Responsibilities of Citizens.* CM(99)76. Strasbourg: Council of Europe. *www.coe.int*

Council of Europe (1999b) Recommendation (1401) of the Parliamentary Assembly *Education in the responsibilities of the individual.* Strasbourg: Council of Europe. *www.coe.int*

Flekkøy, M. and Kaufman, N. (1997) *The Participation Rights of the Child: rights and responsibilities in family and society.* London: Jessica Kingsley.

Giddens, A. (1998) *The Third Way.* Cambridge: Polity Press.

Ministere De L'Éducation Nationale (1998) *Histoire, Géographie, Education Civique: programmes et accompagnement.* Paris: Centre National de la Documentation Pédagogique.

Osler, A. (1997) *Exclusion from School and Racial Equality.* London: Commission for Racial Equality.

Osler, A. (1998) Human rights, education and racial justice in Britain: rhetoric and reality, in C. Harber (ed.) *Voices for Democracy: a North-South dialogue on education for sustainable democracy.* Education Now: Ticknell.

Osler, A. (2000a) Children's rights, responsibilities and understandings of school discipline. *Research Papers in Education* 15 (1), 49-67.

Osler, A. (2000b) The Crick Report: difference, equality and racial justice. *Curriculum Journal,* 11 (1), 25-37.

Osler, A. and Morrison, M. (2000) *Inspecting Schools for Racial Equality: OFSTED's strengths and weaknesses.* A Report to the Commission for Racial Equality. Stoke on Trent: Trentham.

Osler, A. and Starkey, H. (1996) *Teacher Education and Human Rights.* London: David Fulton.

Osler, A. and Starkey, H. (1998) Children's rights and citizenship: some implications for the management of schools. *The International Journal of Children's Rights* 6, 313-333.

Osler, A. and Starkey, H. (1999) Rights, identities and inclusion: European action programmes as political education. *Oxford Review of Education,* 25 (1) 199- 215.

Oxfam (1997) A Curriculum for Global Citizenship. Oxford: Oxfam. *www.oxfam.org.uk/coolplanet/teachers/cat2000/*

Parekh, B. (1991) Law torn. *New Statesman and Society,* 14 June.

Qualifications and Curriculum Authority (1999) *The National Curriculum 2000.* London: QCA

Shiman, D. (1999) *Teaching Human Rights.* Denver: Center for Teaching International Relations, University of Denver. Also available at: *www.hrea.org*

Starkey, H. (ed.) (1991) *The Challenge of Human Rights Education.* London: Cassell.

United Nations (1998) *Human Rights Today, A United Nations Priority.* UN briefing papers. *www.un.org/rights/HRToday/*

United Nations High Commission for Refugees (UNHCR) (1994) *Human Rights: the new consensus.* London: Regency Press (Humanity).

Part 3

Practising Democracy

8

Implementing Citizenship Education in a Primary School

David Brown

Despite widespread political support for the introduction of citizenship education into schools in England, following the publication of the Crick Report (QCA, 1998) and the passing of the Human Rights Act, 1998, material support for the development of Citizenship in primary schools has at best been minimal. Although Citizenship is a key new feature of the National Curriculum 2000, the level of priority it is being given can be inferred from the absence of any reference to Citizenship in the new OFSTED inspection framework (1999), which came into effect in January 2000.

This chapter considers ways in which primary schools might develop citizenship education, drawing on the experiences of Mountfields Lodge School in Loughborough where I am headteacher. In particular, I consider how we might most effectively adopt a whole school approach and incorporate Citizenship into the ethos of the school, ensuring that it is part of pupils' overall development. It is critical that these issues are given attention if current efforts to promote Citizenship are to prove more successful than the attempt made a decade ago, when Citizenship was introduced as a cross-curricular theme in the National Curriculum. (NCC, 1990)

Challenges and constraints

When developing effective citizenship education, primary schools need to address three central challenges. These relate to:

- aims and content

- the culture of primary schools and their position in the community

- time constraints.

Aims and content

Carr and Harnett (1996) describe citizenship as 'an essentially contested concept' in the sense that 'criteria governing its use are constantly challenged and disputed'. This is, however, a contest that has largely taken place beyond rather than within schools and which has allowed schools to step back and avoid recognising the importance of citizenship education to their work.

The promotion of 'good citizenship' is not a new role for schools. Nevertheless, a key challenge facing educators is that of reaching consensus on what constitutes a good citizen. Much of the current discourse focuses on the need to achieve a balance between rights and responsibilities in children's education, yet this concern is far from new. Some eighty years ago this debate was also taking place, but at that time the author of a publication entitled *The British Citizen* (Peddie, 1920) identified work in the colonies as one of the responsibilities for which children should be prepared. In the guidance on education for citizenship issued by the National Curriculum Council in 1990, the 'essential components' for citizenship education reflected the political perspectives and preoccupations of the government of the day, with a heavy emphasis on duty, the importance of wealth creation, and the family (NCC, 1990). These examples serve to illustrate changing notions of citizenship, with implications for curriculum aims and content.

The 2000 version of the National Curriculum goes some way towards establishing a 'uncontested common core' (Carr and Harnett, 1996) or consensus. It establishes the broad aim of helping children to be 'responsible and caring citizens capable of contributing to the development of a just society' (QCA, 1999: 11). The framework for Personal, Health and Social Education and Citizenship for primary schools (QCA, 1999) includes the three strands of social and moral responsibility, community involvement and political literacy, recommended by the Crick Report (QCA, 1998).

Other interested bodies are providing further valuable guidance for schools. The Commission for Racial Equality's *Learning for All* (2000) builds on the recommendations of the Stephen Lawrence Inquiry report (Macpherson *et al*, 1999) and the Government's subsequent action plan (Home Office, 1999) linking these to citizenship education. An earlier Oxfam publication *A Curriculum for Global Citizenship* (1997) proposes ways in which values and attitudes, skills, and knowledge and understanding for citizenship can be developed, in a way which complements the Crick model.

The formal curriculum

The Crick Report recommended that learning outcomes for Citizenship would be able to take no more than 5 per cent of curriculum time, linked with PSHE but distinct from it. Significantly, the Citizenship Advisory Group cast some doubt as to the effectiveness of cross curricular teaching. The Crick Report goes on to accept that Citizenship can be taught in combination with other subjects but suggests that the outcomes should be tight enough for both pupil assessment and external inspection. In the National Curriculum 2000 key stage 1 and 2 documents, however, Citizenship remains a non-statutory area.

The National Curriculum non-statutory guidelines for PSHE and Citizenship include many points which have a direct reference to the strands of social and moral responsibility, community involvement and political literacy, suggested by the Crick Report.

The most recent QCA guidelines 'PHSE and Citizenship at key stage 1 and 2' follows very closely the views of its advisory committee. Setting a whole-school framework for PSHE and Citizenship, it proposes what will be a manageable and flexible approach to curriculum based citizenship education. It accepts that schools will already deliver some aspects of the citizenship curriculum. There is also a strong case made for linking with, but being distinguishable from, PHSE. This will be valuable in work with parents, staff and governors.

The QCA guidelines propose three forms of curriculum provision:

* discrete curriculum time
* citizenship through other subjects and
* citizenship through activities and school events.

Each of these provides opportunities for different aspects of the citizenship curriculum. It will be important to ensure that planning for the strands of social and moral responsibility, community involvement and political literacy is made explicit.

The school and the community

Although the period since the Education Reform Act, 1988 has been one of profound change for all schools (relating to school governance, financial frameworks, curriculum, testing and inspection) little has changed in the expectations of relationships within schools. The hierarchical way in which schools are organised has evolved only slowly since the nineteenth century. The 'head's substantial, if not formidable, concentration of power and authority' (Nias *et al*, 1989) may have been tempered by the increased role of parents and governors in school management, but it has been reinforced by a reduction in local education authority (LEA) control and by an increased emphasis on leadership. The rise of 'super heads' who are expected (single-handedly?) to transform failing schools, is an example of this. Changes to existing hierarchical relationships, such as the introduction of school councils or consultations with parents or ancillary workers, are often perceived, with some justification, as risky. The application of citizenship education will challenge the nature of existing relationships.

Schools which view Citizenship as more than an additional aspect of the formal curriculum will need to review their structures and organisation. Progression to what Osler and Starkey (1996) describe as a maximal approach, where the school is a model of the good society, will require organisational changes which permit the development of children's participation skills. A question which is likely to be raised in many staff and governors' meetings is whether the benefits of this form of citizenship education outweigh the threats which such changes pose.

Primary schools are closely tied to their local communities in ways that many secondary schools are not. They are thus more open to scrutiny by the community. Changes in school organisation are generally more visible to the wider community than changes in the school curriculum. Schools may therefore attract adverse publicity for changes in organisation and relationships that may be essential for effective learning for citizenship but which question orthodox views.

Nevertheless, parents, governors and teachers are likely to respond positively if they can see the gains for children. Osler and Starkey (1996) present a model of citizenship education which makes an explicit link between PHSE and Citizenship and highlights the benefits of an approach which places emphasis on both structural/ political and cultural/personal aspects of learning. They identify specific outcomes in schools which have achieved a maximal approach. For example, children in such a school will be able to share their opinions and explain their views. They will understand the decision-making processes open to them in school and take a responsible part in them. This is the realisation of political literacy at primary level.

In support of learning for citizenship it is also possible to make explicit the relationship between the UN Declaration of Human Rights and the experience of children in school. For example, a school which applies Article 5 (prohibition of inhuman or degrading treatment or punishment), will be one which actively combats bullying of children and staff.

If the outcomes which ensue from citizenship education can be expressed in positive, straightforward and immediate terms, it will be possible to begin a process of change which is radically different from earlier attempts to reform relationships in schools. The difference lies in a debate which is inclusive of parents, all staff and governors, as representatives of the community.

There is now a growing awareness that concentration upon narrow standards and testing in primary schools is tending to limit children's experience and threaten their well-being. This is not to detract from the importance of literacy and numeracy, but to acknowledge that they need to be complemented by other knowledge and skills. Evidence of this movement can be seen on the letters pages of the educational and national press and in correspondence to radio programmes. These signs of a changing debate suggest that the climate may be more sympathetic to the development of citizenship education than at any time since the introduction of the National Curriculum.

Time constraints

There is no doubt that the primary curriculum of the 2000 National Curriculum remains over-crowded. Nevertheless, the 2000 curriculum has led many schools and LEA advisers to adopt a more radical approach to curriculum planning. The new programmes of study have aided this process by identifying clear links between subjects and enabling teachers to identify themes as a more practical way of approaching the prescribed content. For example, Leicestershire LEA has supported the work of a team of primary teachers who have worked with LEA advisers and a representative of the Qualifications and Curriculum Authority (QCA). The team has identified ways by which even the formal structure of the literacy strategy can be linked to a more integrated curriculum. The process is still in its early stages but it is by no means a return to a Plowden 'child-centred' model of provision. It may, however, encourage an integrated approach to learning which supports the development of the skills, values and understanding required for effective citizenship education.

A whole school approach to Citizenship

I would describe citizenship education at Mountfields Lodge as embryonic. We have gone some way to promoting appropriate values and dispositions. We encourage the development of some relevant skills and attitudes and we teach some of the key concepts. There are thus some key elements of a citizenship programme in place but we do not have as yet a clearly identified policy for Citizenship, with a supporting planning, monitoring and assessment programme, accepted by governors and staff and supported by the majority of parents.

Our policies towards children's activities are inclusive and we apply equal opportunities procedures. We have developed an anti-bullying policy and challenge racism whenever it arises in school. In many practical respects our children have become guardians of these areas. Many children will point out when they feel that their own or others' experience does not match the stated aims of the school.

Similarly, we have developed some organisational and administrative procedures which allow for the participation of a wide constituency in the decision-making processes in school. This has been an evolutionary process, rather than a clear policy linked to teaching and learning for citizenship and democracy. We will now need to identify the critical elements of a Citizenship programme, determine which of these elements is already in place and what additional provision needs to be made.

The QCA guidelines (1999) suggest ten elements, taken from the National Healthy School Standard, upon which a whole school approach to citizenship may be based:

- leadership, management and change
- policy development
- curriculum planning and resourcing
- teaching and learning
- school culture and environment
- giving pupils a voice
- provision of pupil support services
- staff development, health and welfare
- partnership with parents/carers and local communities
- assessing, recording and reporting pupils' achievement.

In the context of Citizenship it might be appropriate to re-order these elements, particularly to bring the school culture, pupil voices and partnerships with parents and communities to the fore. For each element, it is possible to identify elements of our current provision which will meet the requirements of citizenship education. This activity might usefully be carried out with the participation of staff, governors and parents. The following examples illustrate how we might initiate the process.

School culture and environment

The aims of the school, set out in the prospectus and re-stated in the home and school agreement, state that we work to realise

> ... a school environment in which each child is cared for and respected as an individual; feels secure and gains enjoyment from learning; can reach the highest standards of achievement, social understanding and behaviour; [and] learns to play a confident, responsible and contributing role in the society of which the school is part.

Links can be made with both the UN Convention on the Rights of the Child and to the Council of Europe's (1985) *Recommendation on Teaching and Learning about Human Rights*. An appropriate starting point may be for the school community to re-assess the school's aims and support systems to ensure that they acknowledge fully the rights of children, staff and families.

Leadership, management and change

The relationship between individual members of staff, governors and the external framework within which the school operates is defined, to an extent, by law and by employment practice. There is, however, room within this to re-evaluate the role of the various participants. For example, channels by which individuals and groups contribute to the annual School Development Plan could be revised.

Policy development

The recent practice of the school has been for members of staff and associated governors to draft policies, following working group meetings. These are presented to relevant governors' committees and finally adopted by the governing body. If citizenship education is to make an impact on the whole school it will be essential to extend this process to include as wide a representation as possible.

Staff development

This is an area that is also addressed in the school's aims. Our staff development programme has recently included reviews of the work of support staff and an acknowledgement of their right to expect training and support. Annual personal interviews go some way towards meeting welfare requirements. If we profess an inclusive and consultative approach it will be necessary to apply this to management procedures and to ensure that it covers all categories of staff.

Partnerships with parents/carers and local communities

We included consideration of our links with the local community as part of our recent operational review. Our structures for partnership and participation include representative groups such as the children and staff council, the parent and staff association committee, and the link governors' meeting. Other formal groups include class groups, teams, class representatives and various teacher groups, governors' committees and local organisations. Of course there are also informal groups which are made up of children, parents' groups, and various consultation groups. Such structures continue to evolve and we have a recently established special needs (SEN) support group. It is important to consider the work of these groups in a whole school context.

Assessing, recording and reporting pupils' achievement

Our assessment policy is currently under review. The whole area will be subject to further consideration in the light of developing policies on school self-evaluation and monitoring. The evaluation of children's developing understanding of Citizenship will provide a challenging task.

Ways forward

Burkimsher (1993) states that 'Citizenship Education is intimately tied to the nature of the school'. In this chapter I have provided some examples of how our school will need to adapt its nature in order to provide an appropriate context in which Citizenship can thrive. It will not be a simple process. There will inevitably be those in the school community who will be reluctant to do more than take a minimal approach to Citizenship. It will be necessary to overcome the concerns of those (parents, governors and teachers) who do not as yet recognise the value of the skills and knowledge associated with Citizenship. Teachers have experienced considerable demands and pressures in recent years. Some may need to be persuaded of the value of Citizenship and will need to be made aware of some of the more immediate benefits it will bring to their working lives as well as the longer-term benefits it will offer to children.

All members of the school community will need to be involved to some extent and some may need to be prepared to alter long-held views. It will be important to persuade some that giving children the skills and will to participate in decision-making and 'shape their present as well as the future' (Osler and Starkey, 1996:69) is part of the broader project of raising standards.

Our outline action plan towards developing citizenship education at Mountfields Lodge School is as follows:

First steps

- Briefing meetings for senior staff and governors to consider the Citizenship guidance and summarise the implications for the school.

- Prepare a summary of the Citizenship guidance for all interested parties, including governors' committees, staff groups, parent and staff association, SEN support group.

- Encourage discussion among groups and individuals with a particular interest.

- Promote discussion amongst children, in class and assembly time, of levels of participation and of rules, rights and responsibilities.

Development

- Form a representative group of governors, staff and parents to consider the ten key elements towards developing a whole school approach, as proposed by the Health Education Authority (see above).

- Form a group of subject and age group co-ordinating teachers with representative governors to:

  - consider the overall curriculum programme

  - establish principles for school activities

  - decide upon recommendations for direct Citizenship teaching, class projects, integration with other subjects, and assessment

  - draw up draft scheme of work for assessment.

- Form an initial school council to decide upon representation, agenda and resource issues for a representative school council.

- Convene a school conference to consider the recommendations of these three groups.

- Present recommendations to the school governing body.

Implementation

- Consult with the members of staff and governors whose role may be influenced by the recommendations accepted by the governing body.

- Begin to introduce the changes to the school structure and organisation which are part of the accepted citizenship programme.

- Establish representative school council.

- Integrate Citizenship scheme of work into medium and long term planning process.

- Monitor introduction of the scheme of work.

Time-scale

The time-scale is likely to depend on a number of factors. The planned programme will need to be sufficiently flexible for different aspects to proceed at different rates. The transition from development to implementation is likely to be most successful if it can be timed to coincide with changes in the planing cycle and time-tabling which we anticipate will follow the move to the revised curriculum 2000.

References

Burkimsher, M. (1993) Creating a climate for citizenship education in schools, in: J. Edwards and K. Fogelman (eds.) *Developing Citizenship in the Curriculum.* London: David Fulton.

Carr, W. and Harnett, A. (1996) *Beyond communitarianism: citizenship, politics and education*, in: J. Demaine and H. Entwhistle (eds.) Basingstoke: Macmillan.

Commission for Racial Equality (2000) *Learning for All: standards for racial equality in schools.* London: CRE.

Council of Europe (1985) Recommendation R (85) on Teaching and Learning about Human Rights, reprinted in: A. Osler and H. Starkey (1996) *Teacher Education and Human Rights.* London: David Fulton.

Home Office (1999) *Stephen Lawrence Inquiry: Home Secretary's Action Plan.* London: Home Office.

Macpherson, W. *et al.* (1999) *The Stephen Lawrence Inquiry.* Report of an inquiry by Sir William Macpherson. London: The Stationery Office.

National Curriculum Council (1990) *Education for Citizenship.* York: NCC.

Nias, J., Southworth, G. and Yeomans, R. (1989) *Staff Relationships in the Primary School.* London: Cassell.

OFSTED (1999) *Inspecting Schools: the framework.* London: The Stationery Office.

Osler, A. and Starkey, H. (1996) *Teacher Education and Human Rights.* London: David Fulton.

Oxfam (1997) *A Curriculum for Global Citizenship.* Oxford: Oxfam.

Peddie, J. (1920) *The British Citizen.* London: Blackie and Son.

Qualifications and Curriculum Authority (1998) *Education for Citizenship and the Teaching of Democracy in Schools.* Crick Report. London: QCA.

Qualifications and Curriculum Authority (1999) *The National Curriculum: handbook for primary teachers in England. Key stages 1 and 2.* London: DfEE/QCA.

9

Practising Democracy in two Inner City Schools

Priscilla Alderson

The British Government invited the United Nations Special Rapporteur on the Right to Education to conduct a mission in the United Kingdom during October, 1999 (Tomasevski, 1999). The Special Rapporteur welcomed the Government's initiative in making human rights central to global development, education and relief of poverty. She noted that the Government had committed itself to 'using its influence to seek the realisation of the social and economic rights contained in the Universal Declaration for all the people in the world' (FCO/DFID, 1998).

The Special Rapporteur pointed out, however, discrepancies between Britain's foreign policy and aspects of domestic policy which ignore children's rights. She said that the availability of schools and teachers is not enough. She noted that the Government has 'human rights obligations to make schooling accessible, acceptable and adaptable' (Tomasevski, 1999:13). The Special Rapporteur suggested that the vaguely defined concept 'social exclusion' could be more precisely defined as 'denial of social rights'. The use of 'social exclusion' tends to individualise problems and blame, or at least concentrate on trying to correct excluded individuals, rather than recognising and addressing the 'statal' exclusions and discriminations which oppress them. She also expressed concern about the status of human rights in the Crick Report on citizenship education (QCA, 1998). She said that in the Crick Report, human rights are 'perceived as different from and alien to the rights and freedoms that learners will recognise in their everyday lives [such as] equal opportunities and gender equality' (Tomasevski, 1999:25). 'Individualism and competitiveness as root values clash against solidarity and community' and mutual acceptance (ibid:25). It is a 'paradox' to expect schools 'to instil values of solidarity and individual competitiveness at the same time'. The 1998 Human Rights Act will make a great difference in time; meanwhile the Special Rapporteur sees the UN Convention on the Rights of the Child 1989 (CRC) as 'a particularly well suited starting-point for learners from the youngest ages'. It offers a 'clear and easy identification with its spirit and wording and the immediate possibility of its translation into practice through the creation of a human-rights-friendly school' (Tomasevski, 1999:26).

A research project exploring British children's views about their rights in schools (Alderson, 1999a, 1999b) by means of questionnaires and small discussion groups involving students aged 7 to 17, showed the wisdom of the Special Rapporteur's Report and the adverse effects of denying children's rights in schools. Articles from the CRC, such as the right to respect for the child's worth and dignity; the right to privacy; to develop skills and talents; to express a view in matters which affect the child; were expressed in practical questions about the students' daily experiences. Many students reported not feeling respected as 'they [teachers] make you feel an inch high'; and not being able to trust teachers to keep a secret, or to ensure fair discipline, or to listen to the students' views. Simply having a school council can often seem worse to students, if it is undemocratic, than not having a school council at all (Alderson, in press).

The few published examples of headteachers in Britain who have tried to make their schools more democratic show how hard this task can be (for example, Trafford, 1997). This chapter illustrates, through research in two unusual primary schools, how the Special Rapporteur's concerns can be put into practice in English schools. Highfield School (1997) emphasises democracy as peaceful consultation, listening to and learning from all concerned, everyone having the chance to contribute to policy making which is negotiated and tested before it is agreed. Cleves School (1999) especially attends to non-discrimination and to equal respect and opportunity in gender, ethnicity and ability. Both schools are in very disadvantaged areas and over half their pupils have identified learning difficulties. They both avoid excluding pupils, although many disturbed and distressed children attend them. The following two sections consider how the schools, as the Special Rapporteur advised, alter structures in education which are hostile to difference and disability, and aim to make themselves accessible, acceptable and adaptable.

Creating democratic structures

Some years ago, Highfield Junior School was renowned for being a difficult school and the staff reported mayhem and vandalism. A new headteacher arrived and over five years the school changed and became instead well known for its high standards of positive behaviour. The staff and pupils told the story of this change in a book (Highfield, 1997). The staff began by introducing a firm discipline code. The children agreed they liked feeling safer but 'we'll always cause problems because we don't like adults ordering us to do things'. So the adults and children began to work together on sharing agreements about rules and plans to improve the school. They used methods such as class circle times, when each person has a chance to speak in turn while everyone else listens, sometimes simply as a game, sometimes as a forum for negotiating plans and decisions. The younger children decided the main rules for their class room, the older ones gradually came to think about conventions: 'a rule is a convention if you've made it your own .... it's inside us'.

Circle times were also used to resolve problems such as bullying, when bullies were confronted and asked to explain their case. To ensure that the strategies to prevent bullying worked, some children were appointed as 'bully busters', although this did not continue for long. Instead some children became 'guardian angels', to fly to the rescue of victims and bullies when necessary, and help them to change. The children talked a good deal about feelings and behaviour, through games and more formal lessons, and thereby increased their conscious awareness of self and others, community and solidarity. Each class began to take on the task of resolving behaviour problems, which used to take up most of the headteacher's time. Sometimes classes invited parents to attend a circle time to discuss their child's problems and agree together on positive, non-punitive plans for change.

The circle times worked well for problems within classes, but many problems arise between classes, such as during break time. The staff and children established a school council which also met as a whole school circle time. The council discussed business reported by class representatives, who then reported back to their class circle time and collected new matters to raise at the council. Everyone in the school could feel fairly closely linked to the council, able to raise matters, receive reports, and send further comments back if they were not satisfied. Another crucial method for democratic resolution of problems was the growing use of trained peer mediators and, in time, children in every age group became skilled mediators. The lunch time supervisors, one per 70 children, especially appreciated and relied on the mediators. The children 'help to run the school', fulfilling many useful duties in named posts for which they write job descriptions and apply to be appointed during induction weeks each school year. The staff are keen to involve everyone including difficult children, many of whom become very active and enthusiastic, including some who have been excluded from other schools.

Working for democratic inclusion

Cleves School staff and pupils have also told their story in a book (Cleves, 1999). Cleves is a mainstream school in a local authority with an inclusive policy where every child is welcomed into their local school. Some of the schools include more disabled children than others do. For example, deaf children attend certain mainstream schools where they can actively be members of their deaf community as well as belonging to the general school community where everyone uses some sign language.

Cleves is surrounded by short term housing for several inner city boroughs and there is a continual flow through the school of refugee and asylum seeking children. Twenty-seven languages are spoken. The staff believe that all the structures and detailed practices set up to welcome and educate these children benefit everyone in the school, by alerting staff to each child's individual needs and ensuring there are resources and knowledge to meet a great range of needs. The local authority's support and reallocation of resources, through closing almost all the special schools and making special education integral to mainstream learning, is essential for Cleves School's success (Alderson and Goodey, 1998). The resources include consulting many experts in education, health, social and community services in the borough. The children are aged from 3 to 11 years, and one in ten of them has profound and multiple learning difficulties. There is one teacher and one assistant for every twenty children. In each of the four wings of the beautifully designed school, twelve staff share in team teaching up to 120 children. The children 'direct their own learning' by, for instance, filling in their daily diaries and marking their order of activities. The teaching teams constantly balance each child's individual learning needs with the activities of the whole 'base group' (class of thirty) and the whole wing.

Daily activities show how fully the children take part in democratic inclusion and demonstrate kindness and mutual respect for all regardless of ethnicity or ability. For example, one boy in a wheelchair is able, with the support of other children, to enjoy using the climbing frame and slide in the park adjacent to the school. Another example is the weekly school assemblies where everyone celebrates being together, and which OFSTED inspectors described as 'wonder-full'. One argument in favour of sending disabled children to special schools is to shelter the children from the taunts, bullying and other cruelties of non-disabled children. However, the children at Cleves School show not only that there can be warm friendships and absence of cruel discriminations in mainstream schools but also that it is the children who make inclusion really work, through their relationships and solidarity which adults alone could not orchestrate.

Lessons from the two schools

The two schools illustrate how it is possible to achieve high standards of democratic community in English schools, and in schools in disadvantaged areas. Perhaps there are extra incentives for the staff to experiment in 'failing' schools. Both schools had inspired headteachers but they were not 'top-down super heads' brought in to impose new ideas. These two women were convinced that it is essential to work in solidarity with their staff and pupils; it is illogical to attempt to impose democracy, which can only grow systemically through the contributions of all concerned, albeit with the headteacher's active guidance when overcoming racist, sexist and anti-disability structures and traditions. Both schools were supported by committed governors. The chair of the Cleves governors, for example, who is blind, is convinced of the importance of inclusive education. Although they did not explicitly refer to the UN Convention on the Rights of the Child (CRC), both schools honoured the CRC in spirit, and Highfield emphasised the children's citizenship of their local estate, city, country, 'of Europe and the world'. The staff worked with the pupils to create 'human-rights-friendly schools' and towards realising the UN Special Rapporteur's standards of schools which are 'accessible, acceptable and adaptable'. The examples of Highfield and Cleves suggest that improving schools can only fully be achieved when adults work more equally with children as contributing citizens in democratic school communities.

References

Alderson, P. (1999a) Human rights and democracy in schools. Do they mean more than 'picking up litter and not killing whales'? *International Journal of Children's Rights*, 7:185-205.

Alderson, P. (1999b) Civil rights in schools: the implications for youth policy. *Youth and Policy*, 64:56-72.

Alderson, P. (in press) School students' views on school councils and daily life at school. *Children and Society.*

Alderson, P. and Goodey, C. (1998) *Enabling education: experiences in special and ordinary schools.* London: Tufnell Press.

Cleves School (ed. P. Alderson) (1999) *Learning and inclusion: the Cleves School experience.* London: David Fulton.

Foreign and Commonwealth Office/Department for International Development (1999) *Human Rights Annual Report for 1999*. London: FCO/DFID.

Highfield School (ed. P. Alderson) (1997) *Changing Our School: promoting positive behaviour*. London: Institute of Education/Plymouth: Highfield School.

Qualifications and Curriculum Authority (1988) *Education for Citizenship and the Teaching of Democracy in Schools (Crick Report). Final Report of the Advisory Group on Citizenship*. London: QCA.

Tomasevski K (1999) *Mission to the United Kingdom of Great Britain and Northern Ireland (England) 18-22 October 1999, by the UN Special Rapporteur on the Right to Education*. Geneva: United Nations Economic and Social Council, Commission on Human Rights.

Trafford, B. (1997) *Participation, Power-sharing and School Improvement*. Nottingham: English Heretics Press.

United Nations (1989) *Convention on the Rights of the Child*.

10

Democratic Practice in a Secondary School

Jeremy Cunningham

This chapter is based on reflections on my daily experience as headteacher of John Mason School, Abingdon, a mixed 11-18 comprehensive. It also draws on examples from Carterton Community College, a mixed 11-16 comprehensive, where I was previously headteacher. Over the past 25 years I have been trying to evolve school practice based on the application of human rights through democratic structures (Cunningham, 1991 and 1992).

The people who write advice for teachers usually have a confident, authoritative style: 'I know my stuff; just listen to me and you will know what to do'. Although I have struggled with issues of participation and democracy in school for over twelve years as a headteacher, I cannot write a tidy operating manual. I merely offer some reflections and an admission of some failures. If we want young people to learn that they can have some control over their lives and that they can, collectively, improve the quality of life for themselves and others, we must let them practise. Giving students a real chance to be involved means that they will make mistakes. Coping with the results of these mistakes is an important element of a genuine effort to develop participation. If the response to the mistakes is to regard the whole process as a failure, the game is lost. We teachers make mistakes too; recognition of these helps us and others prepare for next steps.

The school as a community

The school's own vision of itself is the essential foundation of any work in citizenship and participation. What is the school? Whose is it? Is it just a collection of buildings? Does it belong to the head and the teachers? Occasionally parents refer to 'your school' in complaint letters, revealing their basic assumption that we are not part of a collective enterprise. If the students (not pupils) are genuinely to feel that the school is theirs for the time they study there, they have to be told so frequently and explicitly. They have to be included in plans for the future. For example, we share our development plans in outline form with the students, including simplified financial elements. A weekly newsletter for students and parents is the main method of communicating plans and ideas. Assemblies are also often used for letting students know what is going on. The expression of the essential values of the school is summed up in the slogan: High Standards, Happy School, Honourable Service (the style is deliberately Sainsbury not Arnold). 'Honourable Service' was added to counter the consumer approach to education as an individual good to be acquired in the market place. I use the slogan frequently to push out the message that education is a community duty laid on us all to achieve a more just, peaceful world.

Justice and Participation

The school's systems for dealing with offences must be known to be fair and be based on fundamental principles of rights and responsibilities. Being sure of the facts; working for reconciliation and reparation; allowing students to explain themselves; these are very important expressions of a school's and society's values. Unless the members feel that the process is for them rather than done to them, elaborate systems of participation will be flawed at their base. A copy of the Universal Declaration of Human Rights and the United Nations Convention on the Rights of the Child has been distributed for every classroom, to give students reference to the fundamental value-structure for discourse. They can be referred to quickly if there are 'rights clashes', such as freedom of speech versus respect for the religion or ethnicity of others. The last article of the Universal Declaration of Human Rights specifically affirms that no right implies the right to destroy any of the others. Recently, while I was talking to a very responsible student who had overstepped the mark in terms of freedom of speech, he referred to the Universal Declaration. I was pleased that I had a copy on the wall behind my desk and was able to discuss the issue in terms of competing rights and duties.

Most large schools re-scale themselves into small units. The form group, tutor group or subject classroom is the context for the most effective student participation. The fundamental procedures for good group discussion, best of all chaired by a young person, are an essential for everything else. They have usually been well established in primary school, where 'circle time' is a common experience. In the first year of secondary school it is absolutely vital to re-establish these fundamentals for the new social context and new groups. The layout of the classroom into a circle of chairs, the establishment of procedural rules and the avoidance of teacher domination of the discourse are all crucial. In secondary school, surprisingly few teachers know how to avoid leaving students with their aching arms in the air, by simply recording who has indicated a desire to speak and keeping an ordered list. Some teachers find these essentials wearisome. To change a classroom laid out in rows into a circle seems to take a long time if it is unusual and unplanned, but takes little time if everyone knows what to do. No real mutual discussion can take place in the rows of a normal classroom layout.

Our own learning-research group has interviewed and questioned many groups of students about the basic requirements for good learning. One of the key points the students made is the importance of feeling safe from ridicule by other students. Only under these conditions can students admit to what they do not understand or reveal their personal views on important matters. Therefore excellent classroom management and firm, fair discipline is required for everyone to feel empowered to speak. In most classes I watch, generally the same six or seven most confident students take the lion's share of the talk. Teachers become used to the fact that this is so, and that the majority is literally a silent majority. Positive discrimination is sometimes essential if the less confident members are to have some space to talk and be heard. Curiously enough, calling on individuals by name to participate can be liberating for some students who do not like to volunteer but who will answer if asked. Teachers sensitive to the varieties of cultures in a school will know who responds best to which approach.

The context for democratic discussion in our school, like many, is usually Personal and Social Education (PSE) or the key stage 4 Religious Education programme that includes elements of Philosophy and Citizenship. The PSE course is taught by the form tutor. At its best, this approach means that the teacher responsible for many of the most difficult issues is also the one who knows the group best and who has a good idea of the inter-personal relationships within the group. The downside is that some tutors have weak skills in the fundamentals of chairing discussions and in maintaining a culture of mutual respect in the classroom. Team leadership in this area has to be particularly effective if teachers are to be able to support each other in developing some of these crucial classroom management skills. The best tutors use the registration and 'free time' opportunities to help students express themselves and to plan activities together. It is often in these contexts that vital issues of race, gender and class are addressed, because the discussion will have arisen from actual events or disputes. The tutor must have the firm basis of a school value system dedicated to equal opportunities and respect, so as to be able to respond to tensions by allowing dialogue and discussion. This will be particularly true in schools with wide social and ethnic mixes.

Student Representation and Democracy

For students to have some purchase on their own lives in school, they need representative systems. But in society at large, representative democracy appears weak. The community does not know its representatives very well, and often regards them as ear-less and power-less. The same can easily be true in school. The representatives can all too easily turn out to be from the better-off social classes, already confident and articulate. Three or four times a year, we hold 'mass meetings' of the entire year groups of 180 students (six classes). Class representatives make a report on concerns and questions to be read out to the whole year group. The Head of Year organises for minutes to be sent to the School Management and the School Council. These are important occasions for students to be able to check their concerns and complaints against those of other groups, and for the management to gauge how widespread a concern is. However, as the School Council has only two representatives from each year group, there is currently too great a distance between the form group and the Council. In this gap, Year Group councils have developed in two of our Year Groups. They have two representatives from each class and a secretary. In each case they have needed the full support, encouragement and time of the Head of Year, and have met in the lunch break. The more successful one has raised money for charity, organised social and sporting events, and has greatly added to the atmosphere of student initiative and responsibility in the school.

The School Council proper has been through a successful period and a weaker period. In its successful era, it acted on student demands for lockers and for improvements in safety and atmosphere on the buses. It used its moral position to make the headteacher lead changes to school policy. The reasons for its success were partly to be found in the character of its senior officers and their sound understanding of communications and administrative efficiency. They were ably supported by a volunteer teacher who was dedicated to the development of democratic skills.

The headteacher should not be too closely associated with the School Council. This presents a dilemma when it is weak, since I wish to help strengthen it but must not end up controlling it. A termly meeting for the chair, senior officers and supporting teacher is necessary in order to maintain skill levels. The School Council at John Mason has operated an in-house insurance business, and has the right to raise money for itself through, for example, non-uniform days. It can decide how to spend the money to benefit all students. It decides on what charities to support each term or year. It has its own noticeboard, and occasionally uses the weekly newsletter, but its communications back to the students as a whole are weak. It needs to make sure that the good work it does is known about.

Students usually appear to be much more interested in quality of life issues than in curriculum issues. Toilets, food, lockers, homework, dress code, travel, safety, rights, privileges, rules are all perennial items for discussion, suggestion and complaint. Discussion of the curriculum is not actively discouraged, but I think that the pressures of OFSTED inspection and the National Curriculum have reduced student chances to talk about subjects and curriculum balance. It must be admitted that not having another lobbying sector to contend with suits our own very pressured management group. It would be particularly altruistic for us to make great efforts to encourage students to talk about these matters. A School Council at my previous school developed a policy of inviting Heads of Department to talk about their subject and their plans for the future. Sometimes the students found it hard to work out what was on and off limits in these discussions.

John Mason School has a Senior Student Team of eight Year 13 students. It is created partly by election and partly by advice from staff who know the track record of the students in other types of responsibility. It meets weekly with me and takes on leadership projects. So far, the elements directed at the leadership skills of the students themselves have been more successful than their specific projects aimed at working with younger students and building participation projects. Once again communications are a real difficulty to overcome. The Senior Students set up meetings and need to make contact with the students to remind them to come. They have much greater difficulty in reaching the individual student than, say, a member of the office staff.

Successes and challenges

If the senior management has an open and determined policy to encourage participation, it creates a number of informal operations that run alongside the formal representative institutions. These operations involve far more people than the formal approach. They give rise to problems and mistakes as well. Here are some examples:

- a Year 9 production of 'Joseph' was almost entirely planned and carried out by students. It was hugely successful, but we had some health and safety problems associated with the backstage and lighting team.

- Year 10 and 11 Information and Communications Technology monitors are keeping an eye on the computer rooms at lunchtime. One of them was caught abusing his position to create an underground web-page which insulted some teachers.

- Year 10 students are linked with the Year 7 intake and undertaking anti-bullying work. This works well but needs constant leadership time. My efforts to relieve teacher time by arranging for the Senior Student Team to take the leadership have been unsuccessful so far. They do not have the necessary authority or credibility yet.

- Many lunchtime tournaments are organised by the students themselves. These have been highly successful. I am not sure that the organisers receive enough credit for their volunteer actions.

- Year 9 students have volunteered to help in the canteen. This worked well for a few years.

- Library monitors have been so successful that they can keep the library open even when the librarian is away.

- Discos are often organised by the students themselves. Often there are mistakes involving health and safety, ticket sales, or arrangements for supervision. The gains outweigh the losses however.

- Year 12 students run a vending machine business.

The feedback from these operations has to be frequent and supportive. It is no use encouraging them to happen and then coming down like a ton of bricks on the mistakes. The rest of the student body has to hear about the successes and how we proud are of them. It is notable that many of the most active and vocal of our student representatives have 'cut their teeth' on self-help projects.

We send six students to join other students from local schools in the Youth Forum organised by our District Council. They have a chance to discuss important local issues. So far they have found it worthwhile as individuals. Yet again the feedback into the school is the weakest element. Not enough people know what they do, or have the slightest idea whether they have made any difference to our local community.

Listening teachers

Pushing out the message of participation is all very well, but a vital element is formal listening. This is easier said than done. I thought it was a good step forward to organise a questionnaire of all parents about many aspects of our school performance. But when I drafted a similar one for the students, several staff objected. They felt that there is altogether too much listening to students, that they are favoured over the staff, that there has been too much emphasis on rights and not enough on duties. The project is being redesigned so that questionnaires can go out for students, staff and parents in roughly similar formats to bring home the point that each constituency is listened to. Adults in school who are dealing with turbulent adolescents in stressful working environments can be very sensitive to anything that appears to place the students in a superior or more powerful position. Formal 'listening' is high risk at present, where the culture of accountability is often felt as threatening and punitive. The development of performance-related management and pay will make it more difficult to listen to students 'objectively' as many teachers will be afraid of connections being made with their pay.

Values and School Improvement

Developing formal and informal student participation needs clear, confident whole-school values and a willingness to believe that the students themselves can make a real difference to the quality of school life. It costs time and energy, especially when pieces have to be picked up after an accident. However the rewards are great; students develop autonomy and help create an atmosphere of self-confidence which contributes to the improvement of the whole institution.

References

Cunningham, J. (1991) The Human Rights Secondary School in: H. Starkey (ed.) *The Challenge of Human Rights Education.* London: Cassell.

Cunningham, J. (1992) Rights, responsibilities and school ethos in: E. Baglin Jones and N. Jones (eds.) *Education for Citizenship: ideas and perspectives for cross-curricular study.* London: Kogan Page.

11

Schools, Democracy and Violence in South Africa

Clive Harber

South Africa is a violent society. An average of 52 people were murdered each day in South Africa in 1995, giving it a murder rate more than 80 times that of Britain and making South Africa the most violent country in the world outside a war zone (*Weekly Telegraph*, 20 April 1996). A woman is raped in South Africa every 90 seconds. Moreover, relying on the police for help and protection is problematic – a recent study by the Institute for Security Studies revealed that rapes by policemen amount to one every two and a half days (*The Guardian*, 8 September 1999). A number of factors have combined to contribute to this 'culture of violence' – over forty years of gross economic and political inequality; the social dislocation caused by the displacement of whole communities; violent repression by the apartheid State unavoidably precipitating violent resistance to it; the widespread availability of guns; and patriarchal values and behaviours. This chapter sets out the violent context of education in South Africa and then examines two case studies where education for democracy has played a role in attempts to decrease levels of violence.

Education and Violence

Schools have inevitably been affected by violence. Kadar Asmal, newly appointed as Minister of Education after the 1999 general election, expressed dismay at the high level of violence in many South African schools (Motala *et al*, 1999:12). The daily press in South Africa regularly carries articles on violence affecting schools, as the following titles of articles indicate: 'Children See Teachers Gunned Down'; 'Schools Soft Targets for Gunmen'; 'Police Rescue Besieged School from Rampaging Pupils'; 'Three in Court Over Principal's Shooting' (*The Mercury*, 3 February 1999, 30 August 1999 and 17 August 1999; *The Star*, 27 September 1999). In a survey of the schools in Durban (Griggs, 1997), it was found that in nine out of the ten, gang-related violence was a major problem and that security measures were seriously inadequate. A quarterly review of education in South Africa noted the irony that

> ... while the world was riveted to media coverage of the horrific massacre of thirteen high school students in the United States, the litany of violent acts in South African schools this year alone far surpassed the tragedy in Colorado. (Vally, 1999:8)

A review of literature on violence in urban schools in South Africa (Independent Projects Trust, 1999a) talks of a 'culture of violence' existing in South African schools – a systemic cycle of violence that had its origin in the apartheid years when institutionalised violence became a way of life in homes, schools and communities. Violence became accepted as a powerful means of attaining change and social status was gained by carrying a gun.

One survey of students in 1991 found that 84 per cent had had one of their school mates killed in the violence and 87 per cent reported having been directly and personally affected by violence while at school (Nzimande and Thusi, 1998). In the townships violence is exacerbated by poverty and young people often lack self-esteem and personal confidence so that, in a context where positive role models are few, crime, including violent crime, becomes more attractive. Many South African youth have been victims of violence and are therefore both desensitised and acculturated to it as a way of life. One researcher asked young men in Alexandria Township 'Why is it so easy to kill?' and received the reply: 'We are used to people dying. We see death every day, we no longer fear death. To us death has become a way of life' (Motsei cited in Independent Projects Trust, 1999a).

While the violence of the surrounding society impinges on schools, often through organised gangs coming onto school premises, schools themselves have also helped to reproduce violence. Schools in South Africa have traditionally been authoritarian institutions stressing obedience, conformity and passivity (Christie, 1991). The most tangible manifestation of this authoritarianism was the widespread use of officially sanctioned violence against children in the form of corporal punishment (Holdstock, 1990). Corporal punishment is now illegal in South Africa, but is still commonly used and still supported by many parents and students (Morrell, 1999) and, in KwaZulu Natal, by the Minister of Education herself, despite the fact that

> Numerous studies have shown that far from curbing violence, corporal punishment in fact encourages antisocial aggression, vandalism and perpetuates the cycle of violence. (Vally, 1999: 9)

A recent survey of 750 school students in KwaZulu Natal (Morrell, 1999) found some interesting contradictions. Among African students from township schools in the survey there was a strong public endorsement of corporal punishment. However, the majority of the very same students whose public discourse supported corporal punishment said that they felt schools have also contributed to violence by insufficiently combating the climate of fear created by racism and sexism. A report by the South African Human Rights Commission found that racism was still widespread in schools and that:

> schools have no mechanisms to challenge and stimulate the unlearning of ingrained prejudices, as well as transform the minds of learners. Educators exhibit little or no commitment to constructing a learning environment free from discrimination and prejudice ... Four years after the miracle of 1994, school playgrounds are battlegrounds between black and white schoolgoers. (Vally and Dalamba, 1999: preface)

One of the authors of the report was quoted to the effect that he was 'appalled by the intensity and prevalence of racist and violent thinking' (Garson, 1999).

In terms of gender, the Government's Gender and Equity Task team, which reported at the end of 1997, found widespread evidence of sexual harassment and violence in the education system (Wolpe *et al*, 1997). A recent survey revealed that one in three Johannesburg schoolgirls has been raped or sexually assaulted but that just twelve per cent knew that sexual abuse is illegal. In the same survey more than one in ten schoolboys admitted to having raped or sexually assaulted a girl. Nearly half said they believe a girl means yes when she says no, while sixteen per cent believed girls enjoyed being raped and almost on third said the victims 'ask for it' (McGreal, 1999).

Education and Democracy
In South Africa an educational policy framework now exists which sets out to encourage schools to counter the legacy of violence through the promotion of democratic values, human rights and peaceful conflict resolution (Department of Education and Training, 1995). Under the South African Schools Act 1996 all secondary schools must now have a democratically elected learner representative council which also provides student representation on the school's governing body. In terms of policy this is often described as a radical paradigm shift from the previously authoritarian system of education, but although official intentions are good, the problem is predictably one of implementation. While formal structures of representation may be established in schools, it is a lot more difficult to establish a culture of democratic and peaceful behaviour, given the circumstances outlined in the above section. The remainder of this chapter deals with two case studies. Both demonstrate progress and therefore provide significant pointers to the way ahead, albeit in a still very problematic broader context.

The first case study is of a previously all white girls' school which had desegregated in the early 1990s, but which on the eve of Independence in 1994 was marked by racial tension and conflict among students. During 1995 and 1996 the headteacher led a process of democratisation which involved not only introducing more democratic decision-making structures into the school but also involving staff, students and parents in training workshops to learn the skills, roles and values that would be required in the new system. All members of the school were involved in drafting a new code of conduct and set of school rules which were then owned by the whole school community. The resulting values and rules were strongly based on democratic and non-racist principles. Examples of these rules included 'be open-minded and respect each others' cultures and beliefs'; 'practise tolerance, openness and patience'; 'resolve conflict constructively'; 'express yourself honestly but tactfully'; and 'listen to others' viewpoints'. Interviews with staff and students suggested that as communication improved there was less tension and frustration in the school. There was much less physical and verbal violence, and particularly a dramatic decrease in racist comments. This case study of democratic transition within one school highlights a number of key lessons:

- the process of change must be overt and carefully planned

- it must involve the whole school community

- it must involve the examination of basic values

- staff and students must be consciously prepared for the new roles and responsibilities that democracy brings

- schools must be clear about the difference between *laissez-faire* and democracy

- it is a difficult, unsettling and time-consuming task. (Harber, 1998)

The second case study concerns Independent Projects Trust (IPT), a non-governmental organisation established in 1990, that works with teachers, students, school governing bodies, teacher education institutions and government education officials to assist them in developing effective conflict management skills and democratic processes of negotiation and compromise. Evaluations of IPT's work highlight the success of these methods (Foulis and Anderson, 1995; IPT, 1997) but there has been an increasing awareness within the organisation that teaching conflict management skills is necessary but not sufficient to combat the problem of violence in schools (Caine and Matthews, 1998). IPT has therefore played a leading role in facilitating an alliance of public, private and non-governmental organisations, including the police, to address violence in schools.

This venture is known as Community Alliance for Safe Schools (CASS).

IPT, under the auspices of CASS, has produced a practical guide for school governing bodies on creating a safer school. A key aspect of this is the need to encourage and develop democratic school management and classroom practice in order to create a supportive school environment based on participation, ownership and responsibility. They fear that students might otherwise be alienated from the school and contribute to the problem (Independent Projects Trust, 1999b). The guide was used as part of a pilot project with a cluster of three schools in Durban, to investigate whether intervention in the form of workshop based training involving staff, students and parents, coupled with mutual support between the co-operating schools, can reduce crime and violence.

An evaluation of the pilot project (Harber, 2000) suggests that it has been successful in reducing crime and violence and, in particular, the fear of crime and violence. However, it was clear that outside intervention is necessary to provide the catalyst to help schools to address security issues, collaborate with each other and plan for greater security. Moreover, schools are often marked by a culture where teachers work as individuals for much of the time and it is evident that the schools concerned were not familiar with co-operative and group problem solving approaches to issues – such as security. It is also clear that the workshops have provided a valuable bridge between the police and the schools. Previously, schools rarely co-operated with the police and were unclear about the role and powers of the police in regard to school security. To some extent this is the result of a historical perception of the police as the enemy responsible for enforcing the policies of the apartheid State.

It was also clear from discussions at the workshops that participants from the schools were unfamiliar with arguments, evidence and techniques concerning the operation of democratic forms of education. This is not particularly surprising given the history of South Africa, but it is a problem as there are school policy, management and practice issues that have to be understood and internalised as part of the process of democratising a school. There is an existing body of theory, knowledge and evidence reflected in a literature that needs to be made readily available in a digestible manner if schools are to develop democratically. Questions and discussion at the workshop on issues that emerged, such as: the nature of democracy in a school; teaching controversial issues; the cognitive maturity of students; handling home-school value conflicts; the skills and values to be developed and the teaching methods to be used, confirmed that the participants had not experienced such debates in a planned manner before.

Conclusion

It is clear from the two case studies that South African schools are not helpless in the face of violence and that education for democracy is an important element in helping to combat violence. However, teachers, students and other members of governing bodies need further help in developing their knowledge, understanding, skills and values in relation to education for democracy and this should now be an important priority in both in-service and initial teacher education.

References

Caine, G. and Matthews, I. (1998) Education for Conflict Resolution in KwaZulu Natal, South Africa, in: C. Harber (ed.) *Voices for Democracy : a North-South dialogue on education for sustainable democracy*. Nottingham: Education Now/ British Council.

Christie, P. (1991) *The Right to Learn*. Johannesburg: SACHED/Ravan.

Department of Education and Training (1995) *White Paper on Education and Training*. Pretoria: Department of Education and Training.

Foulis, C-A., and Anderson, D. (1995) *Evaluation of the SMART Programme with the IPT*. Durban: Olive.

Garson, P. (1999) 'At the End of the Rainbow'. *Mail and Guardian*, 12-18 March.

Griggs, R. (1997) *Children at Risk: the security situation in Durban schools*. Durban: Independent Projects Trust.

Harber, C. (1998) Desegregation, racial conflict and education for democracy in the new South Africa : a case study of institutional change. *International Review of Education*, 18 (3): 247-254.

Harber, C. (2000) Protecting Your School from Crime and Violence: skills for creating a safe school – evaluation of a one year programme. Durban: Unpublished Report for IPT.

Holdstock, T. (1990) Violence in schools: discipline, in: B.McKendrick and W. Hoffman (eds.) *People and Violence in South Africa*. Oxford: Oxford University Press.

Independent Projects Trust (1997) *Annual Report for the Period March 1997-March 1998 for SMART Project.* Durban: IPT.

Independent Projects Trust (1999a) *The Experience Review of Interventions and Programmes Dealing with Youth Violence in Urban Schools in South Africa.* Durban: IPT.

Independent Projects Trust (1999b) *Protecting Your School from Violence and Crime: guidelines for principals and school governing bodies.* Durban: IPT.

McGreal, C. (1999) 'Child Rape Shock for South Africa's Establishment'. *The Guardian*, 8 September.

Morrell, R. (1999) Beating Corporal Punishment: race, masculinity and educational discipline in the schools of Durban, South Africa. Paper presented at the Voices in Gender and Education Conference, Warwick, UK, March 1999.

Motala, S., Vally, S. and Modiba, M. (1999) A Call to Action : A Review of Minister K.Asmal's Educational Priorities *Quarterly Review of Education and Training in South Africa*, 6 (3): 1-32.

Nzimande, B.and Thusi, S. (1998) Children of War: the impact of political violence on schooling in KwaZulu Natal, in: *Democratic Governance of Public Schooling in South Africa.* Durban:University of Natal Education Policy Unit.

Vally, S. (1999) Teachers in South Africa : Between Fiscal Austerity and Getting Learning Right, *Quarterly Review of Education and Training in South Africa* 6 (2), 1-19.

Vally, S. and Dalamba, Y. (1999) *Racism, Racial Integration and Desegregation in South African Public Secondary Schools.* Johannesburg: South African Human Rights Commission.

Wolpe, A-M., Quinlan, O. and Martinez, L. (1997) *Gender Equity in Education: Report of the Gender Equity Task Team.* Pretoria: Department of Education and Training.

12

Meeting the Challenge of Inclusion: human rights education to improve relationships in a boys' secondary school

Charlotte Carter

This chapter draws on an action research project conducted in an all boys' comprehensive school in the English West Midlands. The work developed from personal concerns with aspects of the school ethos and a singular, pre-determined masculine identity which appeared to inform every aspect of school life (Osler, 1997). Both seemed to incite intolerance and hostility which in turn were regulated primarily by further conflict and reprisal. The frequency of conflict appeared simultaneously to dilute the potency of aggression while confirming among staff the necessity of a tough stance against disruption.

The climate of conflict was in dissonance with the school's mission statement which aimed: 'to create and sustain a happy and caring learning community where all members are valued for what they are and what they might become'.

My efforts to challenge discrepancies between this projected image and actual school life were viewed as impertinent and naive. Nevertheless, I became confident that school relationships could be improved by the utilisation of a human rights framework. I acted on the basis that:

...the world is malleable, not immutable, and [schools] should be teaching how in practice human beings can unite and mobilise and fight to get things changed. (Richardson, 1991: 7)

The subsequent work was referenced by the United Nations Convention on the Rights of the Child 1989 (CRC). It avoided the undue paternalism which appeared to pervade the school, providing instead a frame of reference that is child-centred and pertains directly to students as subjects (Verhellen, 1993 and this volume). The Convention provides for the consistent and non-ideological operation of children's rights (Cantwell, 1992; Osler, 1994). It also promotes student participation, and regards how students 'think, feel and do' as pivotal in developing mutual understanding and reciprocity (Starkey, 1987). Non-participation can be used as an excuse for over-protectiveness and control (Wringe, 1996).

Research in action

The project consisted of two discrete phases, run sequentially. Initially a small group of self-referred students met for seven months; data was provided from observation and collective memory work. This acted as a spring-board for the subsequent phase where a form group completed a modified, four week programme with their tutor. This chapter focuses on the experiences of phase one.

Initially, to increase my awareness of student perceptions, I distributed a questionnaire across the cohort of 120 students for whom I had responsibility. It asked whether individuals would like help in solving problems. Having examined the responses, I convened a group of ten students to examine the potential of new practices. Our meetings followed a common structure within a clearly defined group contract. Sessions began with an ice-breaker, followed by circle time, a main activity and de-briefing and a final game. The work was divided into three phases, examining:

- the individual student and his position at school
- relationships, rights and responsibilities

- how individuals benefit from working together.

From within the safety of the group, I responded to the students' concerns. My objectives were:

- to encourage the participants to feel good about themselves and to value one another
- to encourage affirmation
- to validate the participants' identities
- to get the students to reflect on their existing relationships and behaviours
- to enable participants to experience the benefits of co-operation
- to provide them with the skills to act more effectively for themselves.

Play was an essential component. Firstly, it helped to foster team-work and gave co-operation credibility. In particular, games were important in maintaining pace and a sense of challenge which provided an alternative outlet for energies which might otherwise have turned aggressive. Secondly, it allowed the group to examine choices knowing that mistakes were acceptable, even welcomed (Hopper, 1995). A favourite was *Koosh Balls,* in which students co-operate to ensure the smooth passage of balls across a circle. To be successful they needed to maintain good eye contact, establishing a suitable pace for everyone.

The challenge of small-scale intervention
The participants found it difficult to create a new culture within the existing climate of the school. The majority of the school population was not involved and would not be changing their behaviour. Outside the group sessions, most of the students said it was easy to become de-skilled or to simply take up their old mantle. Indeed, some of the group felt a little unwilling to use their new skills because they said they were conscious of peer pressure and possible ridicule. However, others tried to implement the new ideas and said they did notice changes in their relationships.

Each member of the group had different motives for joining although they shared the desire to become proactive in school life. As one student explained:

> We have had enough of how things are going, the pupils don't see any change in the problems that the school tries to sort out, so we would like to try to sort them out for ourselves... rather than being told what to do.

To respond to this need for change it was necessary to address four common characteristics:

- disaffection with the existing school ethos

- low self-esteem

- a deficit in interpersonal skills

- a capacity to be reflective.

Disaffection with the existing school ethos

While the school held high expectations of how the students should behave, the students had not been consulted and the potential for including them within what Cunningham (this volume) calls 'the school's own vision of itself' had not been exploited. As far as the participants were concerned, rules were simply a given rather than a framework for living.

It seemed that the necessity for purpose had become a justification for authoritarianism in the school. Participation was seen as undesirable and potentially destabilising. In practice the school appeared to operate from the negative assumption that students would transgress. As one participant commented:

> ..the school just expects us to do wrong and that's the way we get to be involved in what happens... great! It hardly makes you want to get involved when out of the blue they might ask you what you think.

The implicit assumption was that students could not be trusted. One participant commented that 'They [teachers] seem to think we are totally selfish and want to wreck the school ...'

Since the notion of the school as a community had little personal meaning for the participants, they felt disaffected – confused by a context where justice, equality and dignity were inconsistent (Starkey, 1986; Carter 2000). They described how, on occasion, staff would use threats, derogatory names and sharp humour as a means of control and in so doing showed scant respect for the students (Askew and Ross, 1988; Connell, 1989). Yet while overtly authoritarian in their classrooms, some teachers adopted a minimalist presence outside, offering the students inadequate support. Some participants perceived these staff even to condone explicit bullying (Best and Starkey, 1995).

Low self-esteem

Despite their apparently gregarious facades it became evident during the early sessions that the participants lacked self-confidence. They frequently spoke about 'not being good enough' to be valued by others and this manifested itself in apprehension and self-doubt. Reinforced by years of non-participation, they felt ill-equipped to articulate their own needs. This was aggravated by their perception of the often loud and apparently confident banter of others (Haywood, 1993). They appeared to be without a strong sense of self and referenced their identities by the fallout from others and their environment. One of the group, an excellent footballer, provided this disparaging self-depiction:

> It isn't always how you want to feel which counts. Your mates are always knocking you... its easier just to see things the way they do and then you don't get disappointed. Say you miss a goal, you still know you are okay really, but the rest of the team might force you to feel bad and then you do.

The participants' self-image was tentative and precariously dependent on their daily negotiation of conflicting information about who they wanted to be and what they were told they were. As a result they were held back by a quagmire of self-doubt and by dependence on others and the school, neither of which was felt to be safe or just.

Without the opportunity to hear themselves and to enter into an exchange of ideas, their voices, rights and identities could not be asserted. Indeed, affirmation was conspicuous by its absence. The participants found sporadic praise capricious and difficult to negotiate, as it was commonly outweighed by prolific criticism. Ultimately this appeared to unsettle school relationships and undermine their identities. Conditioned by the expectation that they would fail, the participants had previously felt it better simply not to try at all. Clearly this further limited opportunities for praise and discouraged others from empathising with them. One participant said:

> I must be rubbish, even my parents are only ever critical of what I do. I can never be good enough whatever I do, why should school be any different?

A deficit in interpersonal skills

While the school projected itself as inclusive, it failed to back the rhetoric with meaningful structural or interpersonal guarantees. Importantly, there appeared to be no formal consideration of whether the students were equipped to interact effectively. The group felt frustrated by a skills deficit which pre-empted choice and led to inappropriate actions. The majority were unhappy with how they responded and felt they were usually ineffective. They could not envisage solving a problem without aggression but they believed it was unfair of the school to use their ineptitude as a reason for precluding participation.

A capacity to be reflective

Students felt they were discouraged from thinking about their actions and only infrequently appreciated that there were choices. This appeared to inhibit personal and interpersonal awareness. In the absence of felt-knowledge, behaviour was referenced by what offered immediate consolation. Students described how competition and self-gratification clouded the process, saying: 'What is the point in doing something if you can't win against the others? What do I get out of it?'

However, by the end of phase one, the students found that:

> It is really challenging working together... everyone has something really good to add to what you have on your own. You just need to think about how.

Outcomes
Actions

The group's activities focused on developing a bank of proactive skills. At times they became anxious to complete tasks, and transcripts of their discussions sometimes revealed elements of disrespect and frustration between students. Within a comparatively short period of time, improvements in collaboration, non-verbal communication and active-listening were discernible. De-briefing was an important element in this as it allowed the students to reflect and discuss their new experiences, recognising the skills employed. It was also a natural opportunity to offer praise and affirmation.

In addition to the games, the sessions focused on joint decision-making exercises. Particularly useful were exercises where the group had to work collectively to piece together a mystery or reach a unanimous decision. This taught them the value of effective communication. They summarised what they had learnt:

> Making eye-contact helps you to concentrate and lets the other person know you are listening; repeating what the other person said shows you heard it right; writing down notes; not shutting off just because you disagree; if you listen to them they are more likely to listen to you; comment on what they say when they have finished; ask questions.

The structure of working in a circle was important in facilitating good dialogue and the students found it easier to focus on each other when they were in this setting, especially during the games and decision-making exercises when there were more variables and greater possibility for distraction.

Reflexivity

The participants found talking about how they made choices very useful; circle time, where much of this work took place, was particularly prized. Reflection reinforced new behaviours and reduced a predisposition to deploy previous patterns of behaviour in times of conflict.

Feelings

Improvements in feelings of self-identity seemed to enhance the relationships within the group. It appeared that unless a student could perceive his own value, he could not claim and enact his rights and responsibilities in a meaningful way and assumed that others were justified in treating him badly. Accordingly, he did not need to respect the rights of others as they would not be respecting his.

For a strong self-identity to develop, the students had to feel that their views and experiences were important. To achieve this they needed to feel safe enough to be open with others. The implementation of the CRC and a group contract both proved invaluable. Within the sessions discrimination was actively discouraged because it caused conflict and aggression. During circle time the group would talk openly about their experiences and this appeared to enable them critically to examine what had happened to them. Other students would provide insights or examples of their experiences of similar problems. The students and I were equally entitled to reprove or affirm the participants when appropriate. Through this process a sense of solidarity developed. In particular, discriminatory comments and actions were not swept to one side but unpacked and reflected on:

> Normally when someone makes a racist comment about me either it is completely ignored or the teachers wait to the end of the lesson and take me to one side and say how awful they feel. That way it just goes on and the others don't get to know what they did was wrong and how it upsets you.

Only when low self-esteem was addressed did it seem that students could begin to accept that other participants were not a threat to them or their entitlement. At this point they began to interact with one another in a more relaxed and natural way:

> For the first time, Miss, I'm okay, I'm not a loser and I can be and do like the others. I think I'm okay and that seems to make them think so a bit more too.

Knowledge

The sessions were important in providing an opportunity for the students to extend their existing knowledge. The small group was an ideal site for this. Its size enabled everyone to share their ideas and perceptions and this made it easier to track how each individual's knowledge developed. The students' comments reflected how the concepts of universality and indivisibility of rights had taken on real meaning through the group's practices. In particular they found their personal circumstances were not being used as an excuse for different experiences. Gradually the group found human rights not simply to be about 'fairness' and 'unfairness' but that they helped to create an important and valuable framework for living.

Conclusion

Despite its small scale and the contradictory environment in which the participants were forced to conduct the majority of their interactions, the study found that human rights education could be meaningfully employed in developing competent individuals. Such proficiency was shown to be not innate but reliant on conscious development within a trusted environment through a strong sense of self. Without this, students were less likely to recognise their capacity to act and were not in a position to make a meaningful contribution. It was through the practice of thinking-in-action that the students experienced felt-knowledge which increased the credibility of rights and identities. Ultimately phase one illustrated how

> ...Inclusive schools and communities are characterised by a sense of security, wherein individuals do not have to struggle to assert their own differing identities but can work for the good of the whole community. Inclusive communities guarantee respect and justice for individuals and groups. (Carter and Osler, 2000)

References

Askew, S. and Ross, C. (1988) *Boys Don't Cry: boys and sexism in the classroom*, Milton Keynes: Open University Press.

Best, F. and Starkey, H. (1995) Violence, schools and society, in: J. Windebank and R. Gunther (eds.) *Violence and Conflict in the Politics and Society of Modern France.* Dyfed: Edwin Mellen Press.

Cantwell, N. (1992) The origins, development and significance of the UN Convention on the Rights of the Child, in: S. Detrick (ed.) *The UN Convention on the Rights of the Child: a guide to the 'Travaux Préparatoires'*. Dordrecht: Martinus Nijhoff.

Carter, C. (2000) Human Rights in Secondary Education: relationships and identities within an all boys' school. Unpublished Ph.D. thesis, University of Birmingham.

Carter, C. and Osler, A (2000) Human rights, identities and conflict management: a study of school culture as experienced through classroom relationships. *Cambridge Journal of Education* 30 (3).

Connell, R. (1989) Cool guys, swots and wimps: the interplay of masculinity and education. *Oxford Review of Education*, 15 (3): 735-51.

Cunningham, J. (2000) Democratic practice in a secondary school, in: A.Osler (ed.) *Citizenship and Democracy in Schools: diversity, identity, equality.* Stoke-on-Trent: Trentham.

Haywood, C. (1993) Using sexuality: an exploration into the fixing of sexuality to make male identities in a mixed sex sixth form. Unpublished M.A. dissertation, University of Warwick.

Hopper, B (1995) Using groups to develop pupils' learning skills, in: R. Best, P. Lang, C. Lodge and C. Watkins (eds.) *Pastoral Care and Personal-Social Education: entitlement and provision*. Lewes: Falmer.

Osler, A. (1994) The UN Convention on the rights of the child: some implications for teacher education. *Educational Review*, 46 (2): 141-50.

Osler, A. (1997) *The Education and Careers of Black Teachers: changing identities, changing lives.* Buckingham: Open University Press.

Richardson, R. (1991) Introduction: a visitor yet part of everyone – the tasks and goals of human rights education, in: H. Starkey (ed.) *The Challenge of Human Rights Education.* London: Cassell.

Starkey, H. (1986) Human Rights: the values for world studies and multicultural education. *Westminster Studies in Education*, 9: 57-66.

Starkey, H. (1987) *Teaching and Learning about Human Rights in Secondary Schools* Strasbourg: Council of Europe, DECS/EGT (87)20.

Verhellen, E. (1993) Children's rights in Europe. *International Journal of Children's Rights*, 1: 357-76.

Verhellen, E. (2000) Children's rights and education, in: A.Osler (ed.) *Citizenship and Democracy in Schools: diversity, identity, equality.* Stoke on Trent: Trentham.

Wringe, C. (1996) Children's welfare rights: a philosopher's view'; in: M. John (ed.) *Children in our charge: the child's right to resources.* London: Jessica Kingsley.

13

'Race', School Exclusions and Human Rights

Maud Blair

A dean explained: These kids need to be out. It's unfair on the rest. My job is like a pilot on a hijacked plane. My job is to throw the hijacker overboard. (Fine, 1991: 50)

The description used by the dean of an American urban school for students who either do not conform or are perceived as non-conforming, provides an important clue to the un-precedented rate of exclusions of students from British schools. This school administrator adopts a language that constructs an image of children as terrorists who put the lives and liberty of other students at risk. Such a description ensures that consensus will be achieved on the sometimes extreme sanctions that are applied in schools. This kind of language appeals to market understandings of what educa-tion is about, the parameters of which are set by the State and which teachers are obliged to follow.

The media has played an important role in producing an image of children who are suspended and expelled from school as 'high-jackers' and who therefore do not conform to normative understand-ings of what a child should be. Such children, sometimes no older than 9 or 10 were being presented in the mid-1990s as 'yobs' (*The Times,* 25 October 1994; *Daily Mail,* 28 August 1996) and 'thugs' (*Daily Mirror,* 23 April 1996), as 'horrors' and 'louts' (*The Sun,* 28 August 1996). We were presented with images of 4 year olds who bite and kick and punch and whom the teacher is unable to control (*The Times,* 15 February 1991) – children who thus challenge the public's sense of childhood innocence. Such headlines helped to mould public thinking into the view that society is faced with a new breed of child whose roots lie in the 'evil' that was manifested by the 'freaks of nature' (*Daily Mirror,* 25 November 1993), meaning the 11 year old children who killed toddler James Bulger.

Through the 'cultural technologies' of the media, a consensus is created around the disciplinary actions of schools. Mass expulsion of children from school becomes a symbol of 'youth in crisis' and of a general moral degeneration in society which justifies teachers' refusal to teach the 'troublemakers' (Searle, 1997). Infused in all these images are messages, both subtle and unsubtle, about class, 'race', gender, disability and 'otherness' in general. That if the conditions of teachers' lives and work have been made difficult and teachers feel de-skilled and disempowered, this must of necessity impact on students' experiences of school, is conveniently buried under the new priorities of the 'punishment culture'.

'Race' and Ethnicity in Schools

The demonisation of children within the education system is, however, not new to black communities. Whilst the exclusion of black[1] pupils needs to be seen within this context of a negative cultural imaging of children, the *over-representation* of black pupils in suspensions and expulsions can only be understood against a background of racism against black people in Britain and continued racialisation of the behaviours of black pupils in schools. Research over the years has revealed the extent to which the 'image' of the black child influences teachers and how this impacts on black students. The concentration of black children in 'disruptive units' between the late 1960s and 1980s (Coard, 1971), and their designation as emotionally and behaviourally difficult, set the tone for relations between teachers and black students and clearly signalled black children as a problem for teachers and for the education system. A study in a West Midlands local authority in 1981 found that teachers' explanations for the disproportionate numbers of ethnic minority group children in 'disruptive units' included a range of pathological explanations such as black children being 'quick to fly off the handle'; that they were 'more difficult to handle'; or that 'West Indian children are lively (sic) and their liveliness gets them into trouble because teachers fear liveliness and schools like silence' (*Issues in Race and Education*, 1981:11).

The system of 'bussing'[2] instituted by Sir Edward Boyle, Education Minister in the 1960s, and the placing of black children into units for disruptive children or 'sin-bins', as reported by Coard in 1971, were examples of the problematic relationship that was established between black children and the education system. Several writers have argued that black students in both primary and secondary phases of education are disproportionately criticised and apprehended by teachers (Eggleston *et al*, 1986; Mac an Ghaill, 1988; Tizard *et al*, 1988; Mortimore *et al*, 1988; Smith and Tomlinson, 1989; Wright, 1992; Connolly, 1995; Gillborn, 1990 and 1995).

The Problem of Black Youth

It is, however, adolescents, and more precisely black male youth, that seem to represent 'the enemy within' around whom 'moral panics' have been constructed in the everyday discourses of schools. Negative representations of black youth as being a group that threatened the social order of Britain began in the 1970s when the first substantial number of young black people born in Britain began to assert themselves and refused to accept the assimilationist tendencies of their parents. The British tabloid press presented the urban disturbances of the 1980s as confirming the view that black young people were representative of a lawless culture which was both 'un-British' and threatening. A black youth identity was being constructed via media discourses of 'blacks' whose 'unpredictable' and 'volatile' nature was apt to erupt into 'race riots' (Solomos, 1988); as 'muggers' (Hall *et al*, 1978), preying, as Enoch Powell saw it, on helpless old ladies. This discourse was re-inforced in academic studies where black youth were reported as having 'a penchant for violence' (cf.Cashmore and Troyna, 1982) and realised through police harassment which became part of the routine experience of, especially, black males (Gilroy, 1987; Gordon, 1988).

The 1990s saw no release from this kind of assault on the identities of young black people. In 1995, the image of the 'black mugger' was revived by Sir Paul Condon, the Metropolitan Commissioner of Police. Thus the essential '*criminality*' of black people and of black males was being reproduced and re-inforced in the social psyche. The representation of black males as having 'particular tendencies' or drives and inclinations, as possessing 'dangerous proclivities', has justified their closer surveillance by the police and in school; their expulsion from school and their constant presence before the criminal justice system (Scraton *et al*, 1991). It is not, therefore, the crime but the criminality that has been the focus of attention. The level of resentment and anger that this leads to is captured in this statement from a black student:

> Teachers don't treat students with respect anyway, but they have a different approach for black students because they think you're a thief, they think you're violent, they think you're a troublemaker, and from these thoughts (pause) just from the way we're dressed we get stereotyped. A black boy with designer jeans and they want to know where he got them. A friend of mine was in the Withdrawal Room and the teacher was saying, making blatant racists statements saying he must have got his expensive clothes from drug money, and that his brother was a thief and his father was a dealer, making racist jokes like that. That's why I argue so much with teachers, because they say such things and I can't find it in myself to treat such teachers with respect. (Andrew, 15 years)

In schools, these assumptions reinforced what Gillborn (1990) has described as 'the myth of the Afro-Caribbean challenge' and influenced the tendency for teachers to make subjective interpretations of the behaviours of black students.

'Race' and Human Rights

That black pupils are over-represented in school suspensions and expulsions is an outcome of these racialised images of black pupils and their families and of the resulting negative relationships between white teachers and black pupils (Wright, 1987; Gillborn, 1990; Osler, 1997; Sewell, 1997). The implications of this for black young people are far-reaching and resonate with the experiences of minority peoples of colour throughout the Western world. A report by the National Association for the Care and Resettlement of

Offenders (NACRO, 1998) establishes a clear link between suspensions and expulsions from school and the criminal justice system. Similar links have been reported in the USA (Jones and Myrant, 1991) where African-American and Latino students are over-represented in school drop-out rates. This over-representation is replicated within the prison system. Tonry (1995) records that incarceration rates in the USA are seven times higher for black people than for white. According to Hanrahan, it is estimated that: 'at the current rate of incarceration, by 2010, the majority of all African-American men between the ages of 18 and 40 will be in prison' (1998: 33).

Similarly, although black people account for less than six per cent of the British population, they comprise eleven per cent of the male and twenty per cent of the female prison population. It has been estimated that:

> on current trends, nearly one in ten young black men will have received a custodial sentence before his twenty-first birthday, double the proportion of his white peers. (Cavadino and Dignan, 1997: 274)

This, they add, is despite the fact that there is no evidence that black people commit more crime than other groups, whereas there is abundant evidence that black people experience differential treatment within the criminal justice system (see also Worrall, 1997).

Conclusion

The long-term effects of expelling pupils from school seem to have little if any impact on disciplinary decisions taken in schools. Although it is not denied that some pupils do create problems for teachers and other pupils in school, the question must still be raised as to whether expulsion is the best solution and for whom. The connection between suspensions, expulsions and the criminal justice system has been well demonstrated and needs to be part of the serious reflection that should take place when considering disciplinary measures against students. In a context in which black and other ethnic minority groups face differential treatment within the criminal justice system, the implications for them raise serious human rights concerns. Teachers in general are clearly not

165

deliberately expelling black students out of malice or a desire to harm them. However, the failure to examine the historical processes which have led to the over-representation of black students in the 'punishment culture', and to act upon this knowledge, implicates schools in the racialised, classed and gendered dimensions of the increasingly voracious prison industry.

References

Cashmore, E. and Troyna, B. (1982) (eds.) *Black Youth in Crisis.* London: Allen and Unwin.

Cavadino, M. and Dignan, J. (1997) *The Penal System: an introduction.* London: Sage.

Coard, B. (1971) *How the West Indian Child is made Educationally Sub-Normal in the British School System.* London: New Beacon Books.

Connolly, P. (1995) Boys will be Boys? Racism, Sexuality and the Construction of Masculine Identities amongst Infant Boys, in: J. Holland and M. Blair (eds.) *Debates and Issues in Feminist Research and Pedagogy.* Clevedon: Multilingual Matters

Eggleston, S.J., Dunn, D.K. and Anjali, M. (1986) *Education for Some: The educational and vocational experiences of 15-18 year old members of ethnic minority groups.* Stoke on Trent: Trentham.

Fine, M. (1991) *Framing Dropouts: notes on the politics of an urban public high school.* New York: SUNY Press.

Gillborn, D. (1990) *'Race', Ethnicity and Education.* London: Unwin Hyman.

Gillborn, D. (1995) Racism and Exclusions from School: case studies in the denial of educational opportunities (Paper prepared for the European Conference on Educational Research (ECER). University of Bath.

Gilroy, P. (1987) *There Ain't No Black in the Union Jack.* London: Hutchinson.

Gordon, P. (1988) Black people and the criminal law: rhetoric and reality. *International Journal of Sociology of Law,* 16: 295-313.

Hall, S., Critcher, C., Jefferson, T., Clarke, J. and Roberts, B. (1978) *Policing the Crisis: mugging, the State, and law and order.* New York: Holmes and Meier.

Hanrahan, N. (1998), Media bows to power: Will Mumia's voice be silenced forever? in D. Burton-Rose (ed.) *The Celling of America.* Monroe, Maine: Common Courage Press.

Issues in Race and Education (1981) No 34, Autumn.

Jones, A. and Myrant, M. (1991) *Trends and Issues 91: Education and Criminal Justice in Illinois.* Chicago: Illinois Criminal Justice Information Authority.

Mac an Ghaill, M. (1988) *Young Gifted and Black: student-teacher relations in the schooling of black youth.* Milton Keynes: Open University Press.

Mortimore, P., Sammons, P., Stoll, P., Lewis, D. and Ecob, R. (1988) *School Matters: the junior years.* Wells: Open Books.

National Association for the Care and Resettlement of Offenders (1998) *Children, Schools and Crime*. London: NACRO.

Osler, A. (1997) *Exclusion from School and Racial Equality.* London: Commission for Racial Equality.

Scraton, P., Sim, J. and Skidmore, P. (1991) *Prisons Under Protest*. Buckingham: Open University Press.

Searle, C. (1997) Demagoguery in Process: authoritarian populism, the press and school exclusions. *Forum* 39 (1): 14-19.

Sewell, T. (1997) *Black Masculinity and Schooling: how Black boys survive modern schooling*. Stoke on Trent: Trentham.

Smith, D. and Tomlinson, S. (1989) *The School Effect: a study of multiracial comprehensives*. London: Policy Studies Institute.

Solomos, J. (1988) *Black Youth, Racism and the State*. Cambridge University Press.

Tizard, B., Blatchford, P., Burke, J., Farquhar, C. and Plewis, I. (1988) *Young Children at School in the Inner City*. Hove: Lawrence Erlbaum Associates.

Tonry, M.H. (1995) *Malign Neglect: race, crime and punishment in America*. New York: Oxford University Press.

Worrall, A. (1997) *Punishment in the Community: the future of criminal justice*. London/New York: Longman.

Wright, C. (1987) Black students-white teachers in: B. Troyna (ed.) *Racial Inequality in Education*. London: Routledge.

Wright, C. (1992) Early education: multiracial primary school classrooms in: D. Gill, B. Mayor and M. Blair (eds.) *Racism in Education, Structures and Strategies*. London: Sage.

Notes

1. I use the term black to refer to peoples of African, Caribbean and dual (black and white) heritage

2. Ethnic Minority group children were dispersed to schools outside their local area in order to avoid having 30 per cent or more 'immigrant' children in any one school.

14

The Children's Parliament in Rajasthan: a model for learning about democracy

Mary John

The Children's Parliament in rural Rajasthan, India, forms an integral part of a much larger system of rural sustainability that has some quite innovative features in which democratic practices are fostered and encouraged. It embodies the values of the villages within which it operates and with which the Barefoot College of Tilonia has a dynamic and supportive relationship (John, 2000).

The Barefoot College

Rajasthan is a semi-arid State in North West India. It has a population of approximately 23 million men and 21 million women (according to the 1991 census) and covers overall an area of 342,239 square kilometres. Most people survive on subsistence farming and manual labour. Illiteracy is a problem, with around 45 per cent of males and 80 per cent of females illiterate. More than half the children of school age (6-14) do not attend school and the majority of these are girls. Rajasthan is divided into 58 blocks consisting of 37, 890 villages. Tilonia, the village in which the Barefoot College is located, is one of the 110 villages in Silora Block and is about two hours drive west from the magical 'pink city' of Jaipur.

Work in the Silora Block started in the early seventies, initially with a two year ground water survey of the 110 villages by Sanjit ('Bunker') Roy, later the founding Director of the Social Work and Research Centre (SWRC) or the Barefoot College – as it came to be known. Gradually health and education programmes and later work in rural industries and agriculture were included in innovative programmes of development for the villages.

Empowerment of the local villagers in the interests of rural sustainability became the cornerstone of the Social Work and Research Centre which began in Tilonia in 1972. The visionary 'Bunker' Roy wanted to break away from the traditional Indian social work tradition which had an urban, middle class and academic orientation. Initially the focus was on economic and technical services to the villages in, for example: the provision and maintenance of solar panels; replacing the dependence on kerosene which had had to be laboriously collected each day by the women; and the training of existing rural midwives in hygienic practices, developing them into more general paramedics to work in their own villages. The Barefoot College believed in capacity building with existing human resources.

A system of training the trainers was set up in the Barefoot College, where local villagers trained other villagers in the skills needed to support these technological breakthroughs in water, energy, health and finally education. Throughout all this work anyone regardless of caste, class or gender was eligible for any staff position. Living and eating together in the college was a new experience for many who came from villages where caste hierarchies were rigid. In keeping with this emphasis on equality, all the Barefoot College's programmes emphasise collective decision-making skills.

The Night Schools

Such thinking led to the development of the Night Schools – and eventually to the Children's Parliament which grew logically out of them. A typical working day for many children in this region begins shortly after dawn with household chores, collecting water and wood, before setting off for work in the fields looking after cattle or doing agricultural tasks – a long day that ends around dusk. Family survival depends on the labours of every member, so sending the children to school is out of the question. The Barefoot College, collectively with the villagers, developed the Night Schools idea which uniquely fitted the educational needs of these children and the time they had available for study after work. The school day and school holidays of the formal education system were unsuitable; the school curriculum had an urban bias; the language of instruction was unfamiliar in the daily life of rural children; often the schools were not within a reasonable daily walking distance for young children. These factors marginalised many rural children from any engagement in the educational process.

The Barefoot College emphasised learning from doing.

> The importance of education lies not in paper qualifications or exams but in achieving the skills that guarantee the sustainable development of rural communities. (O'Brien, 1996)

The emphasis in Tilonia's education programmes sought solutions inside the community itself in a concerted effort to tap its human resource potential.

> This meant modifying existing non-formal pedagogical methods and strengthening the concepts of the Barefoot educators... the importance of the Night School as a nucleus of awareness-building began to emerge. (Roy, 1982)

The community felt that what was needed were learning opportunities that would develop some literacy and numeracy skills, partly for reasons to do with rural sustainability and also to protect them from being exploited by the literate. The learning process should enable the beneficiaries to serve their communities rather than seek individual gain and prosperity. A relevant education that did not alienate children from their surroundings was required. Local staff – the Night School teachers, who have generally completed their 8th grade – come from the villages where they work. This is highly important both for the relevance of what they teach and for their ongoing involvement and dialogues with parents. Girls would not have been allowed to attend the Night Schools if the teachers were not known to their parents. Training of Night School teachers takes two years and is followed by a programme of continuing professional development to further strengthen their classroom skills.

The Children's Parliament (*Bel Sansad*)

From these Night Schools the idea of the Children's Parliament emerged. Innovations in education, it was felt, should serve to make children feel equal and responsible members of society regardless of caste, gender or economic situation. The idea of the Parliament was to challenge and widen children's thinking. Previously their views had not been considered important. Moreover, in a community where the caste system disappears only slowly, many of their opinions had been shaped within their own caste. The Barefoot College staff were anxious that the children's education should expose them to other points of view, with opportunities for discussion. Up to a point the Night Schools did so, but this was given focus and taken further beyond the village through the *Bel Sansad* or Parliament.

The Children's Parliament is the first of its kind anywhere in that children exercise real power through it. Children from each of the sixty or so Night Schools in the district of Ajmer which are attended by about 2500 children (aged between 6-14) are engaged in properly constituted elections for their own Members of Parliament. The experiment was initially launched as a way of teaching the children about politics and the electoral process and has now been copied in various ways in nine other states across India. The rules governing the elections are as follows:

- only children registered as voters are allowed to stand for elections or vote
- candidates should know how to read and write
- thirty eight per cent of seats are reserved for girls
- nomination forms should be accompanied by identification cards and sanction letters from parents and the relevant Village Education Committee
- elections are monitored by the Village Education Committees.

To be eligible to stand as a Cabinet Minister young people have to have attained Standard or Level 3 and above – the same is true for Ministers of State but the rules are a little more flexible if the candidates are girls (after O'Brien, 1996).

There are seventeen seats in the Parliament. Elections to the Parliament serve to teach all the children about the value of recognising good candidates on the merit of their views and commitment regardless of caste, class or gender. The candidates represent two parties: *Ujala* (meaning Light) and *Guaval* (meaning Shepherd). The elected Members – who are aged between 11 and 14 – meet every two months. They elect Ministers – a Prime Minister, a Speaker, a Minister for Transport, Education, Health, Women and for the Environment. The adults function as civil servants servicing this Parliament. The meetings are vigorous and lively, the Members being questioned on each of their activities and responsibilities. The duties of elected representatives are as follows:

- to recruit children to enrol in the Night Schools

- to take attendance every day in the schools – including teacher attendance

- to report on their visits to other Night Schools or other site inspections or visits

- to write to the respective Ministers and Secretaries, should any problem arise or come to their notice in a school

- to attend the meetings of the Village Education Committee and their activities

- to be informed and report on the facilities (especially with regard to health and drinking water) within their village

- to plan out a budget and submit expenses for the running of the Government

- to discuss and decide on all issues taken up at State Assemblies and in Parliament

- to take disciplinary action against any Minister not attending meetings regularly

- to see that elections are conducted in all schools that may have missed out on them. (O'Brien, 1996)

Problems arising in the various villages are reported to the Parliament. The children, for instance, report truant teachers and any matter of local concern or disquiet about local services for deliberation and further enquiry. Each Minister is supposed to visit a number of schools each year and report on the quality of the teaching, attendance levels, the availability and suitability of the equipment and whether the records are being properly kept. The MPs have the power to govern all the schools in this district and to fire teachers who, on the basis of detailed investigation following a complaint, are thought not to be doing their job. They can also apply pressure for further improvements in the village – such as solar power for villages not yet provided with it, or water pumps in areas they think ought to have one. They also organise cultural and leisure activities such as children's festivals. Children through this Parliament are fully involved in every aspect of daily life.

Listening to the views of Members is a very important and educational part of the proceedings. The Speaker of the Parliament in 1996 said:

> Being a good Speaker means giving other children the chance to address Parliament and generally air an opinion without adults butting in: ...if you start speaking what will we learn? There was a meeting last year where we had a workshop and we were doing the Parliamentary budgets. Adults talked a lot and they did not give us a chance to speak. I do not think that that should be allowed.

When asked whether the Parliament is strong enough to bring about change the Prime Minister – a young girl – said:

> What we decide is what happens. We want to see that our schools are well equipped and that all children are attending. And, if the school is well equipped but the children are not studying, then there is something wrong... Sometimes a teacher is a tyrant and doesn't handle the children well or even beats them. We report things like this to our Education Co-ordinator. (The Independent Magazine 4 May, 1996)

The remarkable thing about the Parliament is that children do indeed have considerable power in a society which is regarded as highly traditional and patriarchal.

Initially there was some resistance to children taking their own decisions – based upon a sensed 'lack of respect', respect being a key feature binding people together in the hierarchy of Indian society. There was also considerable unease in the early days about educating girls. The Parliament in some ways represents the reverse thrust of socialisation in that parents, relatives and older villagers learn much from the children about democratic practices, the reasons for these and their importance.

Does the development of the Parliament mean that the children will eventually wish to leave their villages? It seems not, as they say that their ambitions are the fields, goats and their homes. The whole system seems to have strengthened a feeling of belonging and ownership. The Children's Parliament is a valuable means of impressing upon the children the values of responsibility and, as they become actively involved in running their schools, it makes clear to them that with power comes responsibility.

References

John, M.E. (2000) *Children's Rights and Power in a Changing World.* London: Jessica Kingsley.

O'Brien, C. (1996) *The Barefoot College...or knowledge demystified.* Innovations Series. 'Education for all; making it work'. New York: UNESCO.

Roy, A. (1982) *Tilonia's Night Schools: an alternative approach.* Tilonia, Rajasthan: Social Work and Research Centre.

15

The Role of Black Governors

Ian Gittens

Introduction

The Government's proposals for citizenship education aim to encourage young people to develop their skills and knowledge so they can play a key role as active citizens. Such proposals can be realised only if they take account of the cultural pluralism that characterises Britain and embrace the contributions of all cultural groups in influencing what citizenship education should encompass. The kind of local democratic participation encouraged through the work of school governors provides a platform from which local issues and concerns can feed into the processes of educational decision-making. It should permit debate about the purposes of citizenship education and a broader understanding among education professionals about how different groups of people in the wider community experience their citizenship.

This chapter draws on a small-scale qualitative research project which set out to investigate the roles and experiences of black school governors. The findings draw on interviews with fourteen black governors. Their views are contextualised by data gathered over a two year period observing the meetings of the governing bodies of two inner-city schools, both with high proportions of black pupils. By examining black people's perceptions of their roles and responsibilities as school governors it is possible not only to gain insights into their priorities and concerns about education but also to begin to gain a broader understanding of their perception of their roles as citizens within the local community.

In this chapter I use the term 'black' to refer to people of African-Caribbean, African and Asian origins. The term highlights certain common experiences of social and economic disadvantage that may affect the educational experiences and outcomes of people from these groups. I recognise that there are difficulties in applying the term black to such a wide range of people and acknowledge the diversity that exists not only between but also within such groups commonly referred to as 'Asians' and 'African-Caribbeans'. While the term black is commonly applied in Britain, those who use it to describe *themselves* often do so to make a political statement (Figueroa, 1993). It can serve the dual function of demonstrating both pride in a particular identity and of rejecting negative stereotypes and suppositions with which the term black is often associated (Figueroa, 1993; Haw, 1998).

The perceptions of black governors have been largely absent from the body of research evidence on school governors and governing bodies. Much of the research evidence acknowledges the under-representation of black people on governing bodies, but then proceeds to generalise about governors as if they were a homogeneous grouping (Keys and Fernandez, 1990; Golby, 1993; Thody, 1996). Exceptionally, certain writers have highlighted the contribution that black governors can make towards increasing the relevance of school policy to all ethnic communities (Deem *et al*, 1992; Deem, 1989; Tomlinson, 1998; Earley *et al*, 1999).

Responding to community needs

Evidence suggesting black underachievement (DfEE 2000) and disproportionate school exclusion rates have long been issues for black parents, schools and LEAs (Gillborn and Gipps, 1996; Sewell, 1997; Osler and Hill, 1999). The common view is that exclusion from school disproportionately denies black pupils' right to education (Gillborn, 1997; Osler, 1997). Within the framework of school governance, education professionals and politicians are accountable to a lay authority – the school governors (Earley *et al*, 1999). This provides an opportunity for members of the local community to influence school policy and ensure that it takes into account the educational needs of all sections of the community. School governors' arrangements, therefore, are particularly significant for communities vulnerable to the effects of inequality, racism and disadvantage. Black governors in particular have an opportunity of ensuring that issues peculiar to the black community are not overlooked in debates that inform school policy. Black governors are thus able to tackle such issues as differential achievement and exclusion rates through a formal mechanism that brings education professions, parents and community representatives together in discussions about education provision at school level. The constitution of governing bodies implies a partnership that is itself a reflection of the key partners within the education service at local level (Thody, 1996).

A number of the black governors interviewed suggest that currently, neither governors nor education professionals are sufficiently aware of issues relating to the educational needs and experiences of black pupils. Consequently, they suggest that one role adopted by black governors is to bring a 'corrective' perspective to the workings of the governing body, in order to improve the experience and attainment of black pupils. Importantly, they perceive it as their duty to alert the governing body to the issues that impact disproportionately on black pupils. For example, Michael, a parent governor, argues that:

> They [black governors] need to be more persistent in getting concrete answers from teachers and Heads of Departments about the reasons behind low black pupil attainment and find out what the school is doing to address it. Too often they are being fobbed off with an unsatisfactory [response]... which is what tends to happen most of the time.

Nevertheless, the governors in this sample vehemently reject any notion that they should be considered as the governing body's expert on 'race' issues. They argue that black governors should not be the only ones to raise issues that are particular to black pupils. They see such issues as the responsibility of the entire governing body who, they suggest, should be aware of the issues affecting the school.

Black governors have a range of personal and professional roles and identities on which they may draw in exercising their responsibilities as school governors. For example, Angela, a parent governor, explains that in contributing to the governing body, she draws on her experience as a childcare professional, teacher and management trainer. She acknowledges that people from different cultural and professional backgrounds have different kinds of expertise that informs a wide range of educational discussions within the governing body. It is notable that her identity as a black person does not feature in the characteristics she highlights as enabling her to make a meaningful contribution to the governing body's activities.

Some governors believe they are making a contribution to both the school and the community. For example, Dennis, a parent governor, states:

> As a black governor, there is more opportunity to become more involved in the school and community. I have a say in the running of the school and I like to think that I have a positive say and that I represent the wider community, and the [black] community at the decision-making level in the school.

For him, acting as a school governor enables him to play a significant role in the local community and to make a specific contribution to the development of the black community.

The policy context

The Government encourages representatives from all sections of the community to become governors and participate in the decision-making processes within schools. Legislation relating to school governorship (Education Act 1980; Education No. 2 Act 1982; Education Reform Act 1988 (ERA)) changed the composition and roles of governing bodies, and promoted the idea of equal partnership between parents, the local education authority (LEA), and the local community. The Local Management of Schools (LMS) mechanism of the ERA delegated to school governing bodies most of the responsibilities previously delegated to the LEA (DES, 1988).

The legislation embodied the assumption that a governing body covering a single school would have a good understanding of the needs of the school and community. In effect, the governing body manages the school with guidance from the LEA. There is considerable emphasis on the role of governors with knowledge and experience of the dynamics within the local community. Governors' range of responsibilities include school staffing; the control and use of school buildings and also the power to suspend and exclude pupils. The disproportionate school exclusion rates of black pupils make the latter a particular area of concern for black people in their roles as parents and governors.

The effective functioning of the governing body requires a mixture of lay and professional knowledge, skills and expertise (Golby, 1993). Governors are in a position to contribute to dialogue and make the kinds of decisions that are essential for informing the educational process. Therefore, black people in their respective roles as pupils and governors and in keeping with their rights as citizens will influence, and be influenced by, school governor arrangements.

Diversity and decision-making

Various models of governing bodies (Kogan *et al*, 1984; Morley-James, 1989; Shearn *et al*, 1995) show different individuals or groups taking the initiative and influencing the outcome of discussions about the school. The individual governor's formal role is often associated with their capacity as teacher, parent and member of the local community serving on the governing body. While individual governors have the responsibility to convey the views of those they represent, listen to all arguments, weigh them up and come to a conclusion in the interest of the school, their overriding function is to maintain the unity of the governing body (Sallis, 1993a, 1993b). In theory, the broad composition of governing bodies ensures that all interests are represented. However, despite the observed benefits of diversity, governing bodies remain generally unrepresentative of the communities they serve (Hatcher, 1994; Landman, 1999).

A culturally diverse governing body helps to ensure the effective flow of communication between the school and the community it serves. Diverse representation on the governing body also sends out the message that the school is taking steps to address the educational interests of all the stakeholders in the community. Additionally, diversity in the composition of the governing body often links the governing body to other influential groups in the community (Pearce, 1993). This kind of association and collaboration has the potential to secure the variety of skills and perspectives needed to facilitate the interchange of knowledge and ideas that are crucial for educational development. Consequently, a governing body that reflects the range of interests in the locality is likely to develop school policies that are relevant to pupils from all cultural groups.

Recent research has identified non-participation in school governorship as one reason behind poor attainment figures (Earley *et al*, 1999). The black governors in this sample confirm these findings and suggest that school governors influence higher pupil attainment, either by actively encouraging pupils to achieve through their presence in the school or by influencing educators through the work of the governing body. Either way, the prevailing view is that black governors have the potential to influence education and ensure that account is taken of black pupils' needs in the policy process.

Conclusion

The black governors in this sample hold a range of perspectives about the roles of black people on the governing body. In particular, they bring a corrective viewpoint to the system of consultation on what is affecting black pupils' attainment and the incidence of black exclusions. They also promote the role of school governor as a citizenship role open to other black people. They encourage black pupils to achieve academic excellence and attune the governing body to the issues affecting the black community. Generally, black governors see the governing body as a mechanism for dialogue around whole school issues. They overwhelmingly reject the notion that they should be dealing only with issues of 'race'. Nevertheless, a minority reveal that they are often called upon to deal with issues involving black pupils.

It is important to acknowledge that some people and groups experience discrimination in the education system because of characteristics other than their ethnic background and culture. Black governors can help to create a culture of understanding and respect for all forms of diversity. Education professionals and planners may find similar approaches based on differences to be important assets in considering their approaches to citizenship education.

References

Deem, R. (1989) The new school governing bodies: are gender and race on the agenda? *Gender and Education,* 1(3), 247-261.

Deem, R., Brehony, K., Hemmings, S. (1992) Social justice, social divisions and the governing of schools, in: D. Gill, B. Mayor and M. Blair (eds.) *Racism and Education: structures and strategies.* London: Sage.

DES (1988) *Education Reform Act: local management of schools: a report to the DES.* London: HMSO.

DfEE (1998) *Excellence in Schools.* London: The Stationery Office

DfEE (2000) *Race Research for the Future: ethnicity in education, training in the labour market.* Research Topic Paper.

Earley, P. *et al,*. (1999) *Improving the Effectiveness of School Governing Bodies.* London: DfEE.

Figueroa, P. (1993) Cultural diversity, social reality and education in: A. Fyfe and P. Figueroa (eds.) *Education for Cultural Diversity: the challenge for a new era.* London: Routledge.

Gillborn, D. (1997) Racism and Reform: new ethnicities old inequalities? *British Educational Research Journal,* 23(3): 345-360.

Gillborn, D. and Gipps, C. (1996) *Recent research on the achievements of ethnic minority pupils: OFSTED reviews of research.* London: HMSO.

Golby, M. (1993) Parents as School Governors, in: P. Munn, (ed.) *Parents and Schools: customers, managers or partners?* London: Routledge.

Hatcher, R. (1994) Culture, consent and contestation, in: A. Thody (ed.) *School Governors: leaders or followers.* London: Longman.

Haw, K. (1998) *Educating Muslim Girls: shifting discourses.* Buckingham: Open University Press.

Keys, W. and Fernandez, C. (1990) A survey of school governing bodies, in: M. Golby (ed.) *Exeter Papers in School Governorship,* 3, Tiverton, Fairway Publications.

Kogan, M., Johnson. D., Packwood, T. and Whittaker, T. (eds.) (1984) *School Governing Bodies.* London: Heinemann.

Landman, R. (1999) Ethnic majority must put its house in order. *Times Educational Supplement,* 16 April: 13.

Morley-James, R. (1989) Increased responsibilities of governors – aspects of school governance, in: B. Fidler and J. Bowles (eds.) *Effective Local Management of Schools*. London: Longman.

Osler, A. (1997) *Exclusion from School and Racial Equality: research report*. London: Commission for Racial Equality.

Osler, A. and Hill, J. (1999) Exclusion from school and racial equality: an examination of government proposals in the light of recent research evidence. *Cambridge Journal of Education* 29 (1), 33-62.

Pearce, J. (1993) What type of director is best for your school? *Management in Education* 7 (3): 31-32.

Sallis, J. (1993a) *Basics for School Governors*. Network Educational Press.

Sallis, J. (1993b) Working with Governors in: H. Green, (ed.) *The School Management Handbook*. London: Kogan Page.

Sewell, T. (1997) *Black Masculinities and Schooling: how black boys survive modern schooling*. Stoke on Trent: Trentham.

Shearn, D. *et al* (1995) The changing face of school governor responsibilities: a mismatch between government intention and actuality? *School Organisation,* 15(2), 175-188.

Thody, A. (ed.) (1996) *School Governors: leaders or followers*. London: Longman.

Tomlinson, S. (1998) New Inequalities? Educational markets and ethnic minorities [1]. *Race, Ethnicity and Education*, 1 (2), 207-224.

16

Parents, Human Rights and Racial Justice

Seán Carolan

With the implementation of Crick's recommendations on education for citizenship in schools (QCA, 1998), issues of political literacy and democracy in schools have been brought to the forefront of educational policy and practice. It has been argued, however, that Crick's proposals are lacking in a number of respects, in particular, that they miss a golden opportunity to highlight the importance of human rights and responsibilities in education (Tomasevski, 1999; Osler, 2000; Starkey, 2000). Nevertheless, they do represent the basis of what might potentially become effective citizenship education. Although Crick notes the importance of community involvement – mainly stressing voluntary service – his focus is one-sided, emphasising what young people might do in the community. He largely neglects the views and experiences of parents, their opinions on racial justice issues, and how they might become involved in the citizenship education of their children. This chapter presents some of the findings from a recent Ph.D thesis on parental perceptions of human rights education in an inner city primary school which explores these important concerns.

Researching parents' views

The research was conducted over a two year period, from 1996-98. Over one hundred parents were issued with a questionnaire on human rights education, followed up by a series of in-depth interviews. Participants represented a diverse range of cultures and communities, including Vietnamese, African Caribbean, Irish, English, Pakistani and Chinese. Parents from all these groups expressed a strong desire to see issues of racial justice promoted in the primary school curriculum and the school's ethos. They saw race equality as a human rights issue and believed their children should be given the knowledge and skills to challenge racism and discrimination. They also wanted to be more closely engaged in school policy and decision-making.

Initial analysis of the responses to the parental questionnaires identified a number of key areas for further investigation with parents, to explore through interviews. These were:

- parents' own knowledge of human rights
- parents' views on children's understanding of human rights
- human rights and the curriculum
- the school ethos.

All the parents stressed the need for children to have an 'all round' education and become competent in numeracy and literacy but also to gain understanding of social issues. They saw primary schools as experiential places of learning where their children might express themselves and learn within a stimulating environment. Importantly parents stressed the need for children from reception class onwards to be made aware of equalities issues, justice and fairness. They recognised that children learn by example and argued that they need to experience positive team-work and co-operation from an early age.

Parents' knowledge of human rights

Parents themselves had a broad understanding of their rights and responsibilities, and explained that this had been acquired both through their own experience and through the media. They considered the school as an ideal place for simple human rights education to commence. They wanted their children to understand how rights are sometimes violated, and to be given the necessary tools to challenge any infringements of their rights, should this occur. In a society where so many conflicting images are offered of what is 'right' and 'wrong' , where subjective views are so frequently expressed, and where negative stereotypical images are forcefully portrayed in the media, parents are understandably concerned.

Human rights and race equality

When parents were asked about the place of human rights education in the curriculum, different messages emerged. Some felt that issues of race, culture, equality and justice should be regularly covered in all curriculum areas, when and where appropriate. In addition, these issues can discussed throughout the school day whenever examples of pupil behaviour allowed a particular theme to be addressed, such as bullying. Furthermore, a democratic school ethos was regarded as one means of facilitating children's learning, although some parents felt that a subject-specific approach might be more appropriate. By specifically teaching 'citizenship' or whatever the subject area was called, cultural issues, antiracist workshops, practical work on equality, consideration of black and ethnic minority historical figures and/or role models might be considered in depth. By giving these issues a specific slot on the timetable, they would be further highlighted and prioritised. Parents were keen that schools were not simply paying lip-service to antiracist education. They saw race equality as a central feature of education, rather than an optional extra. They continually stressed how crucial it was for schools to be actively promoting, prioritising and teaching within an antiracist framework. This supports the results of Osler and Morrison's study (2000), which recognises that schools need to be engaged in a process of self-evaluation as well as being subject to external inspections on issues of race equality.

Improving communication and participation

Other salient issues ensued from the parental interviews. The notion of cultural understanding and sensitivity was stressed as an area where problems often occurred. Such problems are usually easily rectified through simple discussion and liaison between school and home. An area of concern for a large group of Muslim parents, for example, was the inclusion of pork on the school menu. Only when the management team was made aware of this, was the problem rectified. Vietnamese parents expressed concern that they were being excluded from school-community activities because of language barriers. Accordingly, a Vietnamese classroom assistant was employed, and also acted as a translator for parents. Naturally, each individual school must be allowed to develop and identify its own priorities. In the research school, the issue of community languages and the lack of a consistent policy on the translation of letters and reports is still a problem. What is important is that staff and particularly management teams are made aware of the cultural concerns of parents, and recognise that simple actions can often be effective in resolving problems and improving relations.

As Hornby (2000) states:

> Teachers need to be sufficiently aware of the beliefs and customs of the ethnic groups with which they work to be able to adapt their interventions so that they are culturally appropriate.

This clearly depends on a school developing appropriate channels for communication and consultation.

A democratic and inclusive school

Parental discussion on human rights education also revealed the importance to them of school ethos and democratisation and of role models. Parents emphasised ethos on several occasions, as a vital element in engendering a positive spirit of antiracist education. They also considered ethos to be significant in enabling broader social justice issues to be addressed. Parents stressed that teacher codes of behaviour had marked effects on younger children. If children experienced democratic classroom practice, they would accept this as the norm. This had implications for teaching styles, since an autocratic teacher whose class sits silently for much of the day does not engender a spirit of team-work or community. Conversely, a teacher who is flexible and open to change is considered by children and parents alike as approachable, and is appreciated for it. As one parent put it: 'A classroom has got to be like a second home really'.

Awareness of the individual needs of children and their families must remain a fundamental component of any teacher's role.

A related concern, and one which parents frequently mentioned, is the teacher as role model. In the research school, although the majority of children and families came from ethnic minority backgrounds, only one ethnic minority teacher was employed. A 'professional' black role model was lacking in school, while the majority of ancillary staff were from ethnic minorities. Parents expressed concern about the messaged this conveyed. As one remarked: 'How do you think that makes the children feel?'

Recent statistics highlight the gross under-representation of black and ethnic minority people in teaching. The 1999 Labour Force Survey indicates that only 2.9 per cent of teachers are from ethnic minority backgrounds. The picture is equally worrying when we examine particular localities. In Birmingham for example, figures for the year 2000 show that nearly half Birmingham's school children are from ethnic minorities, whereas this is true of less than a tenth of its teaching force. The implications of this for both teachers and pupils are well documented (Osler, 1997). Interestingly, parents stressed the importance of the employment and retention of greater numbers of ethnic minority teachers as a key factor in combating racist attitudes among young children.

Parents also argued that a teaching force which more closely matched the ethnic composition of the pupil population would facilitate the development of greater tolerance. Groups within school undeniably learn much from one other and mutually benefit by being exposed to a range of cultures, religions, value systems, histories and the like. Focusing on common, shared values, such as those of the Universal Declaration of Human Rights (1948), and underpinning a school's foundation and philosophy with these very rights, leads to a democratic ethos, pervaded by equality and fairness for all, irrespective of socio-economic factors, culture or religion. By adopting simple but effective practices, such as school councils and circle time, pupils may see the tangible benefits that democratic structures nurture.

If schools do not remain vigilant, however, a negative spiral of parental alienation may easily evolve, reinforcing inequality across the board. So it is critical that schools address parental concerns and seek to break down the emotional and practical barriers to effective communication. If left unaddressed, parental concerns about racism, inequality and cultural insensitivity are likely to lead directly to further misunderstanding and inequality.

Conclusion

The development of antiracist education may seem an uphill struggle. However, it takes little effort for schools to change some of their practices and thus ensure a fairer, more democratic school community. Human rights education, used as a tool for social justice, not only combats racism, inequality and unfairness but also empowers all members of the school community: children, parents and teachers alike. If schools are to nurture children to be responsible citizens of tomorrow, they need to confront their own negative stereotypes and practices. This needs to be done not only by individual teachers but by institutions collectively. Only then can schools plan and implement change and this may well prove far simpler than school management perceives it to be. By making changes in line with parents' wishes, schools begin to face up also to their responsibility to promote human rights and race equality. They also develop a spirit of community. The advice on democratic structures advocated in the Schools Council's *The Practical Curriculum* (1981), though nearly twenty years old, still remains as true and valid for schools today as it was then:

> Some values, like those of democracy, tolerance and responsibility, grow only with experience of them. Social education arises from a school's ethos, its organisation and its relation with the community. The way a school organises its staff and pupils and its formal rules, say a great deal about its real values and attitudes. Schools need to practice what they seek to promote (Schools Council, 1981).

It is perhaps of this last sentence that all educators should take most heed.

References

Carolan, S. (2000) Parent, teacher and child perceptions of human rights education: a primary school study. Unpublished Ph.D. thesis, University of Birmingham.

Hornby, G. (2000) *Improving Parental Involvement.* London and New York: Cassell.

Osler, A. (1997) *The Education and Careers of Black Teachers: changing identities, changing lives.* Buckingham: Open University Press.

Osler, A. (2000) The Crick report: difference, equality and racial justice. *The Curriculum Journal,* 11 (1) 25-37.

Osler, A. and Morrison, M. (2000) *Inspecting Schools for Race Equality: OFSTED's strengths and weaknesses. A report for the Commission for Racial Equality.* Stoke on Trent: Trentham.

Qualifications and Curriculum Authority (1998) *Education for Citizenship and the Teaching of Democracy in Schools (The Crick Report).* London: QCA.

Schools Council (1981) *The Practical Curriculum.* London: Methuen Educational.

Starkey, H. (2000) Citizenship education in France and Britain: evolving theories and practices. *The Curriculum Journal,* 11 (1): 39-54.

Tomasevski, K (1999) *Mission to the United Kingdom of Great Britain and Northern Ireland (England) 18-22 October 1999, by the UN Special Rapporteur on the Right to Education.* Geneva: United Nations Economic and Social Council, Commission on Human Rights.

17

The Control of Educational Democracy: International Perspectives

Lynn Davies

The task of this chapter is to examine the interface between national policies on democracy in education and the degree of autonomy encouraged in schools. In doing so, one returns initially to the age-old dilemma of the relationship between the State and the individual, the centre and periphery. Internationally, huge changes in global formations (the collapse of communism, the spread of neo-liberalism, structural adjustment policies) have meant a rethinking of traditional forms of state intervention and control of institutions such as education. Democracy is now being seen as a *condition* of development, not as a cause.

In England, the public is experiencing simultaneously a rise in market-based controls and a call for a drastic revision and tightening of our formal governance: a constitution, a reform of both the House of Lords and the House of Commons and acknowledgement of the impact of the European Convention on Human Rights. The introduction of statutory citizenship education in secondary schools is an example of the tension between imposed national curricula or organisational guidelines and the freedom of schools to determine their own learning paths.

This chapter explores the dilemmas around who should steer the democratisation of education in different national contexts. It begins with a critical examination of four key conceptual fields: community competence; accountability; organisational autonomy; and markets. The question is whether educational democracy – like any democracy – should ideally spring from the grassroots or whether it is too important to be left to different sections or forces within society so should be regulated by the State. The chapter then discusses some policy strategies on democratisation of education in various countries before drawing conclusions about legislation and intervention.

Community competence

I begin with the classic problem of liberal educational theory, as outlined by philosophers such as Amy Gutmann. If the formation of children is handled by the State and its experts, is this political paternalism and therefore anti-democratic? On the other hand, do communities possess the moral will or the administrative competence to build a school system capable of teaching children to participate in democratic communities? Will parents choose to equip their children with the faculties of democratic choice? Gutmann introduces the ideal principle of 'conscious social reproduction': these are communities aspiring to a set of educational practices and authorities which they (citizens) 'have consciously agreed'. They then choose the form of their own social formation. Decentralisation can take priority only when there are 'well-educated local majorities' who can discern sufficient competence among local leaders to place their trust in them. The questions are of course who decides what constitutes 'well-educated' and who delineates 'competence'? In resolving moral conflict, there appear to be parallels with Rawls' (1993) reliance on 'established political procedures [being] reasonably regarded as fair'. This again would merely beg the question of who constitute 'the reasonable'.

Do Marxist accounts resolve this? They would portray the school as serving the economic and social interests of capitalism; the process is seen not as a monolithic enterprise, however, and can be continuously resisted. In this, we go back to Michael Apple (1980) or

Paul Willis (1978). Here students display, through degrees from mild humour to total rejection, a critical consciousness of their situation. This is Willis' classic 'partial penetrations of capitalism'. From such signs of potential for organisation derive Connell *et al*'s (1982) 'organic working-class schools' and Giroux and McLaren's (1989) concept of teachers as 'emancipatory authorities'. The latter are to promote a 'pedagogy of student experience', drawing on such experience as 'referent for critique'. This appears similar to Gutmann: students, when becoming conscious of their economic determination, can freely choose the form of their social formation, with the help of radical intellectuals.

The problem which Gutmann and Connell would acknowledge, however, is the imperfections in this community experience. What of working-class sexism? What of the fact that the extension of democratic control to local school boards in America actually impeded racial desegregation, because of the racist nature of those boards? Hunter (1994) in his historical overview *Rethinking The School* provides a measured critique of both the liberal and Marxist attempts to reconcile such dilemmas. The liberal notion of 'educated' people defining competence becomes but a circular argument. The Marxist explains away the anti-democratic (racist, sexist) tendencies in the working-class as merely their prematurity, because of exploitation and of the division of labour; teachers will then share their experiences as workers, and communities will be transformed by the humanising expertise of teachers. Yet this approach 'replicates the liberal strategy of discounting incompetent democratic decisions as ill-educated'.

> This means that the making of politically competent judgements – that is, those that accord with Marxism's expert analysis of the future form of society – determines what is to count as an historically mature democratic community. At the same time, to avoid the tyranny of expertise, it is the judgement of the historically mature democratic community that determines what counts as political competence...the Marxist reconciliation of competence and democratic choice remain circular and lacking in substantive content. (Hunter, 1994:27)

Hunter goes on to suggest that problematic behaviours of students in school, such as sexism or misconduct, are the direct outcome of the pastoral (often Christian based) disciplines through which the school transforms behaviour into an object of ethical concern and attention.

> If this is so, then the idea that 'transformative intellectuals' can exercise an 'emancipatory authority' based on their pure insight into the future form of human development, begins to look dangerously self-deluding. Under this degree of moral inflation the teacher's role threatens to break free of its professional and civic moorings, drifting into moral grandiloquence and political fantasy. (Hunter, 1994:30)

Perhaps to circumvent such critiques, Gutmann and Thompson later develop the notion of 'deliberative democracy' as a solution to the educational problem of free insight and democratic choice.

> [T]he processes of decision-making that citizens encounter at work and at leisure should seek to cultivate the virtues of deliberation...in any effort to make democracy more deliberative, the single most important institution outside government is the educational system. To prepare their students for citizenship, schools must go beyond teaching literacy and numeracy, though both are of course prerequisites for deliberating about public problems. (Gutmann and Thompson, 1996: 359)

This mirrors the sentiments of the Crick Report in England and Wales (QCA, 1998).

But deliberation is not enough on its own; certain principles need to emerge from or underpin the discussion. In the example of the fundamentalist parents who objected to the content of reading books as conflicting with their religious beliefs and maintained their children should not be taught to make critical judgements, Gutmann and Thompson outline certain principles, such as reciprocity, by which such competing claims would be reconciled, or priority given. Parents cannot claim unconditional authority over the education of some future citizens; no citizen can fairly claim that what constitutes good citizenship is whatever happens to conform to his or her particular religion (Gutmann and Thompson, 1996). Those drawing on principles from conventions on human rights will similarly recognise the value of universalistic principles, such as the right to dignity, or freedom of expression, which can be used to determine relevant behaviours. It is indeed possible to find principles by which everyday dilemmas, competing claims and arguments for freedoms and self-realisations can be measured.

Yet the key question for democratic governance is the point at which such principles are deemed to be sufficiently internalised or regularised to 'permit' local self-governance – or, conversely, what types of control, what technologies, what experts are needed to maintain surveillance over local interests and claims to self-determination. Are 'deliberations' sufficient to enforce the principles, and what lines of accountability make such deliberations transparent?

Accountability

One of the operational definitions of a democratic system is a system that is 'accountable' to various publics. Sklar (1996) distinguishes two principal forms of accountability. First is the accountability of leaders to followers, or rulers to ruled, of office-holders to citizenry, that is, the acknowledgement of the ultimate 'power' of the people – democratic accountability. Second is the obligation of office holders to answer for their actions or decisions to one another – lateral or constitutional accountability. These are mutually reinforcing in their effects.

The lack of such accountability is therefore seen as profoundly non-democratic. Forje (1997) refers to it as a 'missing dimension in African politics'. In a response to Vanhanen's analysis of the international prospects of democracy, he notes:

> Accountable government requires a judiciary separated from the executive. An independent and accessible judiciary should be regarded as one of the essential institutional pillars of modern democracy. (Forje, 1997: 324)

Degrees of failure in accounting range from a simple lack of information to outright corruption in government and judiciary, and the latter is considerably exercising international organisations. The World Bank, 1997 *World Development Report* entitled *The State in a Changing World* devotes a whole chapter to 'Restraining Arbitrary State Action and Corruption' (IBRD, 1997). The report defines corruption as 'the abuse of public power for private gain', and the concern is with the use and abuse of state power, particularly regarding the judiciary and separation of powers, but also lower public officials. It comments finally, however, on the delicate balance to be struck between flexibility and restraint:

> Citizens are demanding more responsive and effective delivery of public services and greater probity in the use of public resources. At the same time, globalization is increasing demands for a more agile state, one that can respond quickly to changing circumstances. These pressures have magnified the state's dilemma: how to check arbitrary decision-making without building rigidities that inhibit innovation and change (International Bank for Reconstruction and Development. (IBRD, 1997: 108)

Accountability and anti-corruption in education face the same problem, and are closely linked to the dilemmas of decentralisation and devolution of control. Corruption in education ranges from financial issues of embezzlement and ghost schools, to examination fraud, to bribery for entrance to school or university (Harber and Davies, 1997). There are both efficiency and morality questions here. In an economic analysis of corruption, Bardhan examines the corruption index of countries and finds that:

> While political competition and democracy can provide some check on the excesses of corruption, the effectiveness of local accountability mechanisms does not have a one-to-one relationship with the general democratic character of a regime ...... in Cuba, criticising Fidel Castro may be illegal, but active vigilance of local communities is quite effective in keeping public health and education officials on their toes. (1997:39)

Weak and fragmented governments, on the other hand, can give rise to a 'regime of decentralised looting' (Bardhan, 1997:38).

Decentralisation is often (dubiously) seen as an indicator of demo-cratisation – but it is clear that such processes should not mean a weakening of the checks and balances by which potential corruption and inefficiency is surfaced, and indeed it could be argued that greater monitoring is needed. Policies to reduce corruption in the education service would probably be uncontentious: independent auditing of accounts, external examining in universities, or checking qualifications of teachers and students. It is the accountability around competence that is more difficult. My key concern is esta-blishing principles by which it can be assessed whether a process of accountability is in fact democratic. Does OFSTED (and similar educational inspection procedures in other countries) constitute a democratic procedure?

Three features appear to stand out for scrutiny: the credibility and legitimacy of the implementers of an inspection or quality control process; the issues chosen to be made transparent; and the publics for whom the accountability is designed. In the case of an inspection process, the first issue, of credibility, might relate to whether inspectors were elected and/or subject to removal by popular consent. The second relates to the criteria by which schools are held accountable and whether these criteria reveal the priorities held important by popular agreement. The third would relate to the audiences for the inspection reports: whether governments, parents or students, and who has the power to act upon them. It would seem doubtful on any of these criteria that OFSTED is democratic: its officials are appointed, are not apparently independent of the executive, and their own mechanisms for scrutiny are not transparent; its criteria are limited and not negotiable; and its final communication is only indirectly to the major clients of education, that is, the students. While OFSTED reports do examine areas of pupil 'responsibility', and do comment very favourably on democratic processes in schools such as school councils, their major performance indicators are not those related to whether the school itself is a democratic community.

The argument therefore returns to the degree to which a community can be self-monitoring (as in school-based self-evaluation) and how far external controls and surveillance are necessary to provide the transparency demanded by the democratic process. The ideal in terms of another principle of democracy, that of participation, would seem to be to move towards a system of accrediting an institution's own audit procedures. Both the objects of scrutiny and the clients of the process need mechanisms for challenge.

Organisational autonomy and intermediary institutions

The notion of 'clients' and 'consumers' of education is part of the neo-liberal agenda which has taken root in many parts of the world – often encouraged or demanded by structural adjustment policies. In terms of policy and practice of democracy, the apparent converse to accountability is deregulation: how far do policies of privatisation or giving autonomy to schools represent greater democratisation?

The World Bank expresses great concern at the effects of the particular democratisation process in Brazil which has shifted resources to local governments who have 'used much of their windfall to increase staffing and launch questionable new projects' (IBRD, 1997: 125). In contrast, the Bank speaks highly of voucher schemes and capitation grants. Its report cites the experience of Chile, which has used the capitation grant system to allow a student to enrol in any school – public or private – which then receives a capitation grant from the State. A pilot voucher scheme in Puerto Rico was so successful that in its second year the number of applicants jumped from 1,600 to 15,500. The Bank points out that public funding for private schools is nothing new, and that in the Netherlands two-thirds of students attend publicly funded private schools. It is keen to point out the pitfalls of vouchers and contracting out, particularly in terms of polarisation and corruption, but looks favourably on competition as a key regulator alongside more formal regulatory devices.

The Bank also analyses the impact of policies of 'contracting out', whether to private firms, or – as in the case of social and educational services – to non-governmental organisations. NGOs of this kind, such as religious bodies or health promotion agencies, can provide particular expertise and commitment. The example of Bolivia is cited, whereby the Government contracted with the church-based Fe y Alegria to manage a certain number of mostly secondary schools. Before doing so, Fe Y Alegria demanded (and received) the right to appoint principals and teachers and to allow teachers to work both the morning and afternoon shifts. Salaries and curriculum remain the same as other schools, but the Bank eulogises:

> The only comparative advantage Fe y Alegria have is an exceptional esprit de corps among students, parents and staff. Teachers and students flock to Fe y Alegria schools, with many families paying extra fees for their children to attend ..... this public-private partnership between government and a religious NGO appears to be so successful that the government is studying it as a possible model for national educational reform. (IBRD, 1997: 90)

Yet elsewhere doubts have been cast on the capacity and impact of NGOs to deliver a liberating education, and there are suspicions of the World Bank's sudden embracing of the ideology. Firoze Manji

(1998) notes how its draconian structural adjustment policies had exacerbated social divisions and that the 'trickle-down' effects had been discredited. Popular dissatisfaction with government policies had led to strikes and demonstrations, so that universities were closed and trade unions and student organisations became targets of repressive legislation. Such widespread opposition resulted in some rethinking by official aid agencies and the multilaterals about how to present the same economic and social programmes with a more 'human face'.

Significant volumes of funds were set aside, aimed at 'mitigating' the 'social dimensions of adjustment'. Yet the services were not to be provided by the State (which had been forced to retrench away from the social sector) but by the ever-willing NGO sector. Manji claims that NGOs have played a pivotal role in the 'depoliticization of poverty'. Most will claim that they are neutral, and that they even-handedly provide assistance to both sides of a conflict; this can be humanitarian in war conditions but in non-critical conditions it merely acts to maintain the existing system of social reproduction.

> The dominant discourse on development was not framed in the language of rights and justice, but in the vocabulary of charity, technical expertise, neutrality, and a deep paternalism (albeit accompanied by the rhetoric of participatory development) which was its syntax. (1998:26)

Clearly, NGOs would fear that protest about government repression would threaten their very existence, or at least their exemptions from tax or duty.

As aid budgets in the North declined, many northern NGOs restructured themselves as 'local NGOs', becoming a direct competitor for aid funds in the local market. The field of development has become big business, and large scale transnational NGOs came into existence with the sole purpose of delivering aid with the 'professionalism' desired by the large aid agencies. In the process, their concerns about rights have become fragmented. There is large discussion about the perceived relevance of 'international' rights conventions to developing countries, a discussion which led to the establishment of the African Charter on Human and Peoples' Rights in 1986 – asserting the collective rights of people as well as environmental rights. However, there is a problem with a 'right' seen as a standard granted in charity from above rather than a standard-bearer around which people rally for the struggle from below.

> The field of human rights has recently found much favour among the official aid agencies. The latter regard support for rights as a means of 'improving good governance', 'promoting democracy' and 'strengthening civil society'... Unfortunately the focus of many human rights organisations has been almost exclusively on agitations to claim civil and political rights. Their work remains focused primarily on the urban areas, leaving unchallenged the structures of power which continue to hold hegemony in the name of customary power. (Manji, 1998: 30)

Manji argues that NGOs should return to their anti-colonial stance which expressed solidarity and the struggle for rights of all peoples. Otherwise they stand impotent and bewildered, as they did when genocide erupted in Rwanda.

Markets

Are then African and Latin American countries different from European ones in their embracing of democracy? It is interesting that in post-Communist countries, democratisation is seen as responding to the new neo-liberal agenda of markets. A conference of the Alliance of Universities of Democracy (AUDEM, 1998), a mainly Eastern Europe/US alliance, saw great enthusiasm for market-driven reforms as well as for the power of technology and international communications as a democratising device. There were inevitably questions surrounding the autonomy of universities and academic freedom. It was instructive that the keynote speaker was from the European Bank for Reconstruction and Development:

> As we now enter the second phase of transition, the EBRD finds that stable market reforms entail not only the broad transformation of the economy, but also the 'establishment and reinforcement of a wide range of market-supported institutions in the government, in the legal system and in the civil society'...the EBRD role is to nudge governments in the right direction by making sure new investment meets the conditions that build market economies and protect the environment. (Shepherd, 1998: 4)

To be sure, Shepherd does distinguish between civil and uncivil society, with the latter characterised by barter, trade in illegal goods and services, and corruption. 'Robust' reformers on the other hand have built a strong foundation of political and economic institutions in support of market-oriented transition (Shepard, 1998: 8). The conference grappled with the degree to which controls were needed to counteract the worst excesses of capitalist systems and public choice theory while maintaining the best features of a social market economy.

What is critical is not to accept current economic and competitive market theories as a 'given', a position which James Porter expounds in his excellent book *Reschooling and the Global Future*. His analysis is that the dominant theory of competitive equilibrium and the free market is a 'partial and inadequate explanation of reality' (Porter, 1999: 30). He quotes Ormerod:

> ...the promotion of the concept that the untrammelled, self sufficient, competitive individual will maximise human welfare, damages deeply the possibility of ever creating a truly affluent cohesive society in which everyone can participate. (1994:221)

Porter shows how the effects of government concentration on nationalistic and economic factors in controlling public services has resulted in a reduction in the role of the State with regard to such traditional democratic concerns as equity, justice, security and welfare.

> It is difficult to avoid the conclusion that those in established positions of power have embraced a particular and largely erroneous economic theory because it consolidates their supremacy and control. (Porter, 1999: 33)

Here we see the links to the earlier discussion of accountability, but it is more than that. Adoption of a faulty model of economics has meant steadily growing divisions in the world, between elites and the dispossessed. Efforts to ameliorate these are marginal and 'are failing to stem the dangerous and ultimately disastrous descent into a world that is so split that many will assume that violence is the only available way to seize wealth or power' (*ibid*.: 39). Porter's is a highly pessimistic but powerful portrayal of the impact of acceptance of global economics and financial markets, and he is realistic about what education and schools could do within these huge movements. The alternatives to neo-liberalist doctrine are the State taking a prominent role in material welfare and growth and in encouraging the development of civil society, and/or an institution-centred approach that builds governance capability across a broad range of fields salient for economic life.

Democratic governments have to reassert their authority by challenging the hegemony of elites who currently control the economic agenda, and freeing basic services such as education and health from the bogus quasi-market theory that has predominated in recent years. For Porter, a truly democratic state requires a vigorous, critical and independent school system, a 'released' education service. This means, in UK, a rolling back of the State, of imposed centralised curriculum, of inspection and of the competition for central funds. Reflexive schools and enhanced and reflexive teacher education are the keys to democratic education. Yet, for the purposes of our discussion, this 'release' implies little or no state direction of the processes towards democracy in education – as with relying on 'the community', will it be enough to leave democratisation to a newly revitalised, autonomous and informed teaching force?

Policy strategies

We can learn, therefore, by examining the way that different countries in transition have managed the process towards democratisation in education. In a previous book (Harber and Davies, 1997) we distinguished various levels of effort, from rhetoric to large scale systemic reform. South Korea, although boasting a democratically elected government, still has a highly authoritarian school system, and can be put into the rhetorical category. Malawi is attempting to introduce new, more participative classroom methods through teacher training, although inspectors may still be more concerned with the good lesson plan than whether children are learning anything (a phenomenon I also noted in Zimbabwe). In India on the other hand, the Night Schools of Rajasthan for children working during the day are proving a key exemplar of grassroots activism, with phenomena such as student parliaments and a breakdown of gender divisions (see John, this volume). Post-independence Namibia is attempting to embark on a programme of democratic reform and learner-centred education across all sectors, demanding such features as active student participation in learning, encouragement of choice, mutual respect and the slogan 'all teachers and learners are both learners and teachers'. The *Users Guide to the Education Code of Conduct* sets out the role for students in school management, with direct representation of sixth formers on school boards along with parents and teachers; below this level, the role of students is consultative rather than representative, with their opinions sought but with no real role in decision-making.

The often cited widest reform appears to be in Colombia, with the Escuela Nueva programme. Here 20,000 of the 27,000 rural schools have been engaged in reform to promote active and reflective learning, the ability to think, analyse, investigate, apply knowledge and improve the children's self-esteem. This is coupled with the development of co-operation and solidarity and of civic, participatory and democratic attitudes. The self-instructional elements introduced into the schools are mirrored in teacher training, so that trainees also have to form committees, engage in self-directed learning and take part in research on the community. Significant improvements have been found not only in teacher-pupil and pupil-pupil relationships but also in academic achievement and in the wider impact on community and adult education.

Clearly, different policies on democratic reform will be appropriate at different stages of a country's history. One cannot make generalisations about the level of State intervention into school decision-making. However, on the basis of the evidence above I would argue that school democracy is too important to be left to chance, rhetoric or possible grass-roots activism – whether in 'developed' or 'developing' nations. The evidence from European countries is that legislation and firm central surveillance are essential to support local efforts at participation. In Denmark for example, the legislation is that all schools should have Student Councils, and there are mechanisms whereby such Councils feed into regional and national councils, so that pupils have a voice in a range of arenas. Unlike UK legislation, students are represented on governing bodies. Interestingly, this takes place in parallel with quite a high level of state funding of private and alternative schools.

Our research on pupil democracy in four European countries (Denmark, Sweden, the Netherlands and Germany) revealed both stronger levels of legislation and higher levels of state or local government financing of pupil participation in decision-making (Davies and Kirkpatrick, 2000). School student unions were not just tolerated but encouraged and financed by the centre, so that there was a place where students could be informed of their rights, trained for participation and where government could consult the views of young people in their policy making. In England, there is no such legislation, and in spite of the new Citizenship curriculum, there is no move to make the teaching of human rights compulsory in schools or teacher training, to insist on school councils, to enable pupils to serve on governing bodies nor to create systematic local or national committees for pupil consultation. Our conclusion is that UK is out of line with the rest of Europe on these issues, and that schools, teachers and pupils who are pursuing democratic ideals will receive rhetorical but not concrete support.

Can educational democracy be legislated for?

To try to draw together all these strands and tensions, a typology of state or private intervention can be drawn up (see Figure 17.1). This has two dimensions, firstly of state policy (centralisation – decentralisation, or direct – indirect) and secondly of the values of democracy (social welfare – market).

The recommendation on which is the more effective depends naturally on the definitions of democracy. Pychova (1998) quotes the statistics that in 1996 as many as 550 definitions of democracy had been identified, – ranging from 'modern liberal', 'post-modern liberal', 'realistic', 'populistic', to 'affirmative' etc. Indicators of democracy are similarly broad-ranging, with Vanhanen (1997), for example, in his huge comparative analysis of 172 countries, identifying the number of students in universities and the levels of literacy as key educational indicators.

My own view tends towards the left hand upper quadrant. Democracy requires strong state institutions and a strongly supported civil society. With an independent judiciary, and separation of powers, the

VALUES OF DEMOCRACY

STATE POLICY	social welfare + + + + + + + + + + + + market	
Centralised or direct + + +	• legislation for student participation and human/children's rights • citizenship curriculum • funding for national youth parliaments • accountability and anti-corruption measures	• public funding for private schools • conditionalities on funding • students as consumers with rights • quango direction • inspection and league tables
+ + + **Decentralised or indirect**	• guidelines for participation • community emphasis • civil society • organic schools • emancipatory intellectuals • identity politics	• contracting out to NGOs • competition • vouchers • parental choice

Figure 17.1: Educational democracy and state interventi

State is in a position to enact enabling legislation which would ensure that the minimum conditions for associative democracy were met in schools and colleges – student representation, school councils, equal rights and mechanisms for grievance. It is not sufficient to count the number of students or percentage of literates as proxies for the development of a democratic society. Such students or literates could well be schooled in narrow or fundamentalist views, with no guarantee that they would use their education to benefit others or benefit the development of a peaceful society. Also, it is not sufficient simply to lay out a framework for deliberative democracy or for the discussion of controversial issues in schools, valuable though those activities are. Unless children and teachers participate in the political process, and learn from mistakes, they will not in my definition be the 'well-educated citizens' who can judge the competence of their rulers. Participation involves learning to take the consequences of a democratic decision – voting someone into office, agreeing a compromise position or realising the implications of a majority view (Davies, 1998).

Weak forms of decentralisation and quasi-government agencies do not provide the controls needed for vigilance for human rights or equity. Hirst and Khilnani point out that

> under the guise of 'administrative modernism' and claims to greater efficiency and accountability, subjects which fell properly within the domain of political control and public scrutiny have been entrusted to 'experts' supposedly more competent to make decisions... the past two decades have witnessed the rise of a new form of 'quasi-government' composed of unelected and weakly accountable bodies who have been granted considerable powers. (1996:3)

Their collection of papers *Reinventing Democracy* casts doubt on public accountability being expressed in measurable performance indicators and managerial terms: if costs cannot be accurately assigned to specific aspects of manufacturing, 'the prospect of doing so in open-ended multivalent public services like nursing or teaching will be hopeless' (Hirst and Khilani, 1996).

Strong state institutions are not just about legislation. The model to watch may well be South Africa, which has a Westminster heritage but also a network of 'State Institutions supporting Democracy' which includes the Public Protector (to investigate government maladministration); a Commission for Gender Equality; an Electoral Commission; an Auditor General; a Commission for the Promotion and Protection of the Right of Cultural, Religious and Linguistic Communities, and a Human Rights Commission (Calland, 1998). This may sound over-bureaucratic, but it is the constitution (missing in UK) not the parliament which reigns supreme, applying horizontally as well as vertically. Reform of schooling has to go carefully to avoid backlash and retrenchment, but South Africa is openly instituting central reforms increasing the power of governing bodies, banning corporal punishment and introducing an outcomes-based curriculum, while at the same time increasing the powers of provincial governments (Harber, 1997).

The relative success mentioned earlier of Chile, on the other hand, regarded as 'exceptional' in the Latin America region for its relative government stability and electoral traditions, nonetheless does not provide easy lessons concerning democracy. The only obvious one is the development of clearly defined boundaries between the State and the private sector, in which the state provides the condition for capitalist development without being subject to the pressure of particular interests. For Pearce (1996), this requires not so much a strong or weak State but a State with *capacity*. Botswana, too, is seen as exceptional in Africa. While a bureaucratic elite dominates the development process, and the State hides behind the Tswana definition of the civil service as non-political, a committed political elite promotes development, and democracy emerges gradually as a result of the interaction between development and local traditions (Holm, 1996).

For transitional states, the contrast then is conventionally between authoritarian democracy and the Fukuyama model of unrestrained liberal democracy. In developing countries, the argument is that the former is the only way to eliminate hunger and poverty, to combine the basic elements of democracy with the continuity and coherence of policy that is required for democratic development. In so-called mature democracies, writers such as Hirst (1994) will argue for

CITIZENSHIP AND DEMOCRACY IN SCHOOLS

'associative democracy', with strong, voluntary, free communities, delivering a decentralised welfare state and regenerating regional economies. The State should withdraw to becoming a 'secondary, but vitally necessary, public power providing accountability, transparency and scrutiny, while 'self-governing civil society becomes the primary feature of society' (1994:26). Yet as Leftwich (1996: 292) points out, 'sustained and effective development can never be reduced to administrative arrangements, or managerial considerations evacuated from politics'.

Conclusion

In the arena of education, we return to the debate outlined at the beginning of this chapter about who is making judgements on whose competence. In England and Wales we see the apparently Hirstian decentralised and self-governing school actually being governed by apparently secondary public powers in the shape of OFSTED and the Teacher Training Agency. From the examination of different policy relationships in different countries, I would argue for the converse: a strong but transparent central state to provide frameworks for principles such as human rights and student participation, together with moves towards self-scrutiny and internal democracies for educational institutions and civil society.

References

Alliance of University of Democracy (1998) Perspectives in Higher Education Reform. *Journal of the Alliance of Universities for Democracy*, Knoxville, Tennessee: University of Tennessee, Vol 7.

Apple, M. (1980) *Education and Power.* Boston: Routledge and Kegan Paul.

Bardhan, P. (1997) *The Role of Governance in Economic Development: a political economy approach.* Paris: OECD.

Calland, R (1998) In Search of a Rich Mosaic, *Citizen,* Autumn.

Connell, R., Ashenden, D., Kessler, S. and Dowsett, G. (1982) *Making the Difference: schools, families and social divisions.* Sydney: Allen and Unwin.

Davies, L. (1998) *School Councils and Pupil Exclusion.* London: School Councils UK.

Davies, L. and Kirkpatrick, G. (2000) *A Review of Pupil Democracy in Europe.* London: Childrens' Rights Alliance.

Forje, J. (1997) Prospects of democracy in the contemporary world, in: T. Vanhanen (ed.) *Prospects of Democracy: a study of 172 countries.* London: Routledge.

Giroux, H. and McLaren, P. (1989) *Critical Pedagogy, the State and Cultural Struggle*. Albany: State University of New York Press.

Guttmann, A. (1987) *Democratic Education. Princeton*, Guildford: Princeton University Press.

Guttmann, A. and Thompson, D. (1996) *Democracy and Diagreement*. Cambridge, Massachussetts: Harvard University Press.

Harber, C. (1997) 'The democratisation of education in post-apartheid South Africa' in: C. Harber, (ed) *Voices for Democracy: a North-South dialogue on education for sustainable democracy*. Nottingham: Education Now/British Council.

Harber, C. and Davies, L. (1997) *School Management and Effectiveness in Developing Countries: the post-bureaucratic school*. London: Cassell.

Hirst, P. (1994) *Associative Democracy: new forms of economic and social governance*. Cambridge: Polity Press.

Hirst, P. and Khilnani, S. (eds.) (1996) *Reinventing Democracy*. Oxford: Blackwell.

Holm, J. (1996) Development, Democracy and Civil Society in Botswana, in: A. Leftwich (ed.) *Democracy and Development*. Cambridge: Polity Press.

Hunter, I. (1994) *Rethinking the School: subjectivity, bureaucracy, criticism*. New South Wales: Allen and Unwin.

International Bank for Reconstruction and Development (1997) *The State in a Changing World 1997 World Development Report*. Washington: World Bank.

John, M. (2000) The Children's Parliament in Rajasthan, in: A. Osler (ed.) *Citizenship and Democracy in Schools: diversity, identity, equality*. Stoke on Trent: Trentham.

Leftwich, A. (ed) (1996) *Democracy and Development*. Cambridge: Polity Press.

Manji, F (1998) The depoliticisation of poverty, in: D.Eade (ed.) *Development and Rights*. Oxford: Oxfam.

Ormerod, P. (1994) *The Death of Economics*. London: Faber and Faber.

Pearce, J. (1996) Chile: a divided society, in: A. Leftwich (ed.) *Democracy and Development*. Cambridge: Polity Press.

Porter, J. (1999) *Reschooling and the Global Future*. Oxford: Symposium Books.

Pychova, I. (1998) Democracy and its impact in some post-communist countries. *Perspectives in Higher Education Reform* 7.

Qualifications and Curriculum Authority (1998) *Education for Citizenship and the Teaching of Democracy in Schools*. Crick Report. London: QCA.

Rawls, J. (1993) *Political Liberalism*. New York: Colombia University Press.

Sklar, R. (1996) Towards a theory of developmental democracy, in: A. Leftwich (ed.) *Democracy and Development*. Cambridge: Polity Press.

Vanhanen, T. (1997) *Prospects of Democracy: a Study of 172 countries*. London: Routledge

Willis, P. (1978) *Learning to Labour: how working class kids get working class jobs*. Farnborough: Saxon House.

Notes on contributors

Dr Priscilla Alderson is Reader in Childhood Studies at the Social Science Research Unit, Institute of Education, University of London.

Dr Maud Blair is a lecturer at the Open University. She is Chair of two courses: Race, Education and Society, and Equality and Difference: Gender Issues in Education.

David Brown is headteacher of Mountfields Lodge Primary School in Loughborough, Leicestershire.

Professor Michael Byram is Director of Higher Degrees in the School of Education, University of Durham

Dr Seán Carolan teaches in a primary school in inner-city Birmingham. He recently completed his PhD on Parent, Teacher and Child Perceptions of Human Rights Education.

Dr Charlotte Carter works for Birmingham Advisory and Support Services. Her PhD, completed in 2000, is entitled: Human Rights in Secondary Education: relationships and identities within an all boys' school.

Jeremy Cunningham is headteacher of John Mason School in Abingdon, Oxfordshire.

Professor Lynn Davies is Director of the Centre for International Education and Research at the University of Birmingham.

Professor Peter Figueroa is in the Research and Graduate School of Education at the University of Southampton.

Ian Gittens is a Senior Research Officer. He is currently writing up his PhD thesis on the roles and experiences of black school governors.

Dr Manuela Guilherme teaches English and English-speaking cultures at secondary school and university levels in Portugal, and is also a teacher trainer. She recently completed her PhD on the cultural dimension of English teaching in Portugal.

Dr Clive Harber is Reader in International Education, School of Education at the University of Birmingham.

Professor Mary John is a developmental psychologist. She is a visiting professor at the University of Exeter, where she was formerly Professor of Education and Deputy Vice Chancellor.

Professor Audrey Osler is Director of the Centre for Citizenship Studies in Education at the University of Leicester.

Robin Richardson is a Director of the INSTED consultancy and was formerly Director of the Runnymede Trust.

Sarah Spencer is Director of the Citizenship and Governance Programme at the Institute for Public Policy Research and a member of the Home Office Task Force on the Human Rights Act.

Dr Hugh Starkey is Staff Tutor for Languages at the Open University.

Professor Eugeen Verhellen is Director of the Children's Rights Centre at the University of Ghent, Belgium.

Index

Advisory Group for the Teaching of Citizenship and Democracy in English schools 21-2
Africa 57, 197, 202, 209
African Charter on Human and Peoples' Rights 100-103, 201
Agenda 21 81, 105
Alderson, P. 28, 126, 128
Alibhasi-Brown, Y. 9
Alliance Israélite Universelle 93-4
Alliance of Universities of Democracy 202
Amnesty International 91
Anderson, D. 147
antiracism 47, 82, 87 see also racism
Apple, M. 194
Asia
  campaigns and laws 79
Askew, S. 155
Asmal, K. 143
Audigier, F. 64-5

Baccarini, E. 53
Bangladeshi community, London 88
Bardhan, P. 198
Bardy, M. 35
Barefoot College, Tilonia 169-172
Bassam, Lord 95
Best, F. 155
Birmingham 189
Blackstone, T. 94
Blair, T. 9
Blum, L. 87
Bolivia 200
Bonnett, A. 12, 13

Botswana 209
Boutros-Ghali, B. 102
Brandt, W. 102
Brislin, R. 70
Brock-Utne, B. 37
Bryam, M. 70, 72, 76
Burkimsher, M. 121
'bussing' 163
Bynoe, I. 30

Caine, G. 147
Callard, R. 209
Canada 26
  Charter of Rights 24
Cantwell, N. 152
Caribbean 57
Carlsson, I. 102
Carr, W. 114
Carter, C. 155, 159
Carterton Community College 133
Cashmore, E. 163
Cassin, R. 93-4, 100
Chang, Peng-Chun 88-9
charity 9, 137
Chile 200, 209
Christie, P. 145
circle time 28, 127-8, 135, 157-8, 189
Citizenship Advisory Group 115
civil rights movement 79, 86, 87
Cleves School 127, 128-130
Clough, N. 6
Coard, B. 162-3
cold war 83
Colombia 205
Commission for Global Governance 102, 103
Commission for Racial Equality 94, 107, 115

Commission on the Future of Multi-Ethnic Britain 79, 84
Community Alliance for Safe Schools 148
comradeship 88
Condon, Sir P. 164
conflict resolution 27, 29, 31, 147
Connell, R. 155, 195
Connolly, P. 163
corporal punishment 20, 145, 209
Council of Europe 6, 64, 91, 120
  Committee of Ministers 41, 100
  Parliamentary Assembly 41, 103
Crick Report 5, 7-8, 11-15, 21-3, 27, 75, 115, 126, 185, 196
Cuba 198
Cunningham, J. 133

Dalamba, Y. 145
Davies, L. 29, 198, 204, 206, 208
Deem, R. 178
Delors, J. 66
Denmark 205-6
Department for Education and Employment (DfEE) 4, 6, 8-9, 21-2, 30, 31, 47
Department for International Development (DfID) 125
'disruptive units' 162-3
devolution 83
Doyé, P. 74, 75

215

Earley, P. 178, 182
Education Act 1980 180
Education No. 2 Act 1982
    180
Education Reform Act 1988
    (ERA) 116, 180
Eggleston, J. 163
Enlightenment tradition 67
Escuela Nueva programme
    205
European Bank for
    Reconstruction and
    Development 202
European Commission 13
European Convention on
    Human Rights 8, 19,
    23-4, 31, 39, 82-4,
    103, 193
European Court of Human
    Rights, Strasbourg 19-
    20
European Social Charter
    103
European Union 64
exclusion
    from school 6, 9-10,
    29, 40, 107, 127,
    chapter 13, 178, 181-2
expulsion
    from school 40

Fernandez, C. 178
Figueroa, P. 5, 59, 61, 63-4,
    66, 71, 74, 178
Fine, M. 161
Flekkøy, M. 107
Foreign and Commonwealth
    Office (FCO) 125
Forje, J. 197
Forum on Values in
    Education in the
    Community 23
Foulis, C-A. 147
Framework Convention for
    the Protection of
    National Minorities
    103
France
    l'affaire des foulards
    80
Fraser, N. 68
Fryer, P. 13

fundamentalism 196, 208
Garson, P. 145
Gender and Equity Task
    team, South Africa
    145
Germany 206
    politische Bildung 75
Giddens A. 68, 100
Gillborn, D. 6, 163, 164,
    178
Gilroy, P. 163
Gipps, C. 6, 178
Giroux, H. 69, 195
Golby, M. 181
Goodey, C. 128
Gordon, P. 163
governors, governing bodies
    116-7, 120, 122-3,
    130, chapter 15, 206
Griggs, R. 144
The Guardian 143
Guilherme, M. 69
Gutmann, A. 194-6

Habermas, J. 67
Hall, S. 67, 163
Harber, C. 147, 148, 198,
    204, 209
Harnett, A. 114
Hatcher, R. 181
Haw, K. 178
Haywood, C. 155
headteachers 28, 38, 116-7,
    126, 127, 130, 133-4,
    146
    and race equality 10
    and school councils
    137
Health Education Authority
    123
Helio, P-L. 35
hidden curriculum 61
Highfield Junior School,
    Plymouth 28, 126-8,
    130
Hill, J. 10, 178
Hirst, P. 208, 209-210
Holden, C. 6
Holdstock, T. 145
Holm, J. 209
Home Office 5, 21, 22

Home Secretary (Jack
    Straw) 19, 20-21, 25,
    81
Homebeats 87
Hopper, B. 153
Hornby, G. 188
Human Rights Act 1998
    113, 126
Human Rights Act 2000
    chapter 2, 81, 95
Human Rights Bill 1997 21
Human Rights Commission
    21
    in Commonwealth
    countries 30-31
Human Rights Watch 91
Humphrey, J.P. 88
Hunter, I. 195-6
Hymes, D. 71

Independent Projects Trust
    (IPT) 144, 147-8
India 57, 204, chapter 14
inspection, inspectors 6, 98,
    198-9, 204 see also
    OFSTED
Institute of Race Relations
    87
Institute of Security Studies
    143
International Bank for
    Reconstruction and
    Development (IBRD)
    198, 200
International Covenant on
    Economic, Social and
    Cultural Rights 38-9,
    41
International Human Rights
    Day 96
Islam 80
    Muslim parents 188
Issues in Race and
    Education 163

John Mason School,
    Abingdon chapter 10
John, M.E. 169
Joint Parliamentary Select
    Committee on Human
    Rights 30
Jones, A. 165

Kaufman, N. 107
Keys, W. 178
Khilnani, S. 208
Kirkpatrick, G. 29, 206
Kogan, M. 181

Labour Force Survey 189
Landman, R. 181
Latin America 202, 209
Lawrence, Stephen Inquiry
    4, 5, 84, 86, 115
Lawronen, E. 35
Le Monde 94
leadership 8, 116, 136, 138-
    9
Leftwich, A. 210
Leicesterhire LEA 118
Lenz, G. 53
Lloyd, C. 12
Local Management of
    Schools (LMS) 180
Lynch, J. 37
Lyotard, J.F. 67

Mac an Ghaill, M. 163
Macpherson Report 4, 5,
    84, 86, 115
Malawi 204
Malik, C.H. 88
Manji, F. 200-202
Marshall, T. H. 49, 50, 56
Marxism 194-5
Matsuura, K. 94-7
Matthews, I. 147
Mayor, F. 28
McGreal, C. 146
McLaren, P. 195
McQuoid, D. 27
media 91, 161-3
Mendus, S. 63
The Mercury 144
Ministère de l'Éducation
    Nationale 97
Mohood, T. 59
Morley-James, R. 181
Morrell, R. 145

Morrison, M. 6, 10, 98, 187
Morsink, J. 80, 88
Mortimore, P. 163
Motala, S. 144

Mountfields Lodge School,
    Loughborough 113-
    124
The Muslim News 9
Myrant, M. 165

Namibia 204-5
National Association for the
    Care and Resettlement
    of Offenders
    (NACRO) 164-5
National Curriculum 3-5, 7,
    75, 97-8
    Citizenship education
    chapter 1, 22, chapter
    8
National Curriculum
    Council 113, 114, 206
National Healthy School
    Standard 119
Nayak, A. 11
The Netherlands 200, 206
New Labour 9
newsletters 134, 137
Nias, J. 116
Night Schools 170-3, 204
non-governmental
    organisations, (NG0s)
    91, 95, 147, 200-202
Northern Ireland 11
    Human Rights
    Commission 30, 31
Nzimande, B. 144

O'Brien, C. 171, 173, 174
O'Brien, M. 11
Office for Standards in
    Education (OFSTED)
    98, 113, 128, 138,
    198-9, 210
Oldfield, A. 49-50, 56
One Nation 81
Organisation of African
    Unity 100-101
Ormerod, P. 203
Osler, A. 3, 5-7, 10-11, 13-
    14, 29, 69-70, 91, 98-
    9, 107, 116-7, 151,
    159, 164, 178, 185,
    187, 189
overseas aid 9
Oxfam 10, 115

Parekh, B. 59, 84, 94
parents 116-7, 120-3, 140,
    178, 181, chapter 16,
    196
Paxman, J. 4
Pearce, J. 182, 209
Peddie, J. 114
Perry, M.J. 51-2
Personal, Social and Health
    Education (PSHE) 3,
    61, 104, 115-7, 136
Phillips, M. 87
Phillips, T. 87
play 153
Plowden report 118
Policy Studies Institute 11
political literacy 5, 12-15,
    116, 117
Porter, J. 203-4
Portugal 74
Powell, E. 163
programmes of study
    citizenship education
    8-9, 22, 47, 91, 97
Puerto Rico 200
Pychova, I. 206

Qualifications and
    Curriculum Authority
    (QCA) 4-5, 7-9, 11-
    12, 22, 47, 75, 97,
    113, 115-6, 118-9,
    126, 185, 196

Race Relations Act 1976
    84, 94
Race Relations Amendment
    Bill 2000 9
racism 15, 54, 59, 61, 79,
    84, 96, 163, 165
    and Crick report 7, 15,
    185
    in Britain 6-9, 13, 59,
    80, 88, 119, 162-4,
    178-9
    in South Africa 145-7
    institutional 4-6, 84-6
Rajasthan chapter 14, 204
Ramphal, S. 102
Ramsaran, C. 5
Rassool, N. 66
Rathenow, H-F. 6
Rawls, J. 194

Richardson, R. 3, 6, 37, 152
Risager, K. 70, 75
Robinson, M. 96
Roosevelt, E. 88-9, 100
Ross, C. 155
Rothemund, A. 6
Rousseau, J-J. 50
Roy, S. 170-1
Runnymede Trust 79
Rwanda 202

Sallis, J. 181
Sanders, P. 94
school councils 61, 106,
    107, 117, 123, 126,
    127, 137-8, 189, 205
Schools Council 190
Scottish Human Rights
    Commission 30
Scottish parliament 11, 83
Scraton, P. 164
Searle, C. 162
Sewell, T. 164, 178
Shearn, D. 181
Shepherd, G.W. 202-3
Shiman, D. 99
Sibbit, R. 88
Sklar, R. 197
Smith, A. D. 49, 50, 51
Smith, D. 163
social exclusion 125
Social Exclusion Unit 9
Social Work and Research
    Centre (SWRC) 170
sociolinguistics 71-2
Solomos, J. 163
Somalia 36
South Africa 26-7, 29-30,
    88, 96, chapter 11,
    208-9
    Human Rights
    Commission 145
South Korea 204
Southworth, G. 116
Spencer, S. 30
Starkey, H. 3, 5-6, 11, 13-
    14, 69, 70, 75, 91, 98-
    9, 107, 116-7, 152,
    155, 185
Straw, J. 19, 25, 81
Sweden 206
Tarrow, N. 37
Tatum, B. 88

Teacher Training Agency
    210
teacher training/education
    6, 42, 149, 205
tenants' organisations 88
'Third way' 100
Thody, A. 179
Thompson, D. 196
Thusi, S. 144
*Times Educational
    Supplement* 10
Tizard, B. 163
Tomasevski, K. 125-6, 185
Tomlinson, S. 163, 178
Tost Planet, M. 76
Trafford, B. 126
Troyna, B. 11, 163
Twine, F. 53

Underground Railroad 87-8
United Nations 79, 92-4,
    99, 102
    Commissioner for
    Human Rights 96
    Committee on the
    Elimination of Racism
    (CERD) 82
    Convention on the
    Rights of the Child
    (CRC) 8-9, 28,
    chapter 3, 98-9, 107,
    120, 126, 130, 152,
    158
    Decade for Human
    Rights Education
    (1995-2004) 41, 91
    Declaration on Social
    Progress and
    Development 92-3
    Educational,
    Scientific and Cultural
    Organisation
    (UNESCO) 28, 39,
    41, 66, 94, 95
    High Commission for
    Refugees (UNHCR)
    37, 92
    Special Rapporteur on
    the Right to Education
    125-6, 130
Third Decade to Combat
    Racism and Racial
    Discrimination 96

Universal Declaration of
    Human Rights 8, 38,
    41, 83, 88, 92, 95, 98-
    100, 103, 108, 117,
    134-5, 189
University of the Western
    Cape, South Africa 27
USA 36
    civil rights movement
    79, 86, 87

Vally, S. 144
Van Gunsteren, H. 48-9, 56
Vanhanen, T. 197, 206
Verhellen, E. 37-8, 42, 152
Vienna Declaration 6, 79,
    92, 93
Voorspoed Primary School,
    Cape Town 29-30

Weekly Telegraph 143
Welsh assembly 11, 83
Wexler, P. 48, 66
Williams, Baroness 21
Williams, R 52
Willis, P. 195
Wolpe, A-M. 145
Women's Institute 9
Wood, A. 6
World Bank 197-8, 200
World Conference Against
    Racism 2001 96
World War II 83
Wright, C. 163, 164
Wringe, C. 152

Yeomans, R. 116
Yoshida, T. 70
Young, I. 67

Zarate, G. 72
Zimbabwe 204